THERAPEUTIC ADVENTURES
WITH AUTISTIC CHILDREN

T0385330

of related interest

Teaching Social Skills Through Sketch Comedy and Improv Games
A Social Theatre® Approach for Kids and Teens including
those with ASD, ADHD, and Anxiety
Shawn Amador
ISBN 978 1 78592 800 0
eISBN 978 1 78450 820 3

A Practical Guide to Happiness in Children
and Teens on the Autism Spectrum
A Positive Psychology Approach
Victoria Honeybourne
ISBN 978 1 78592 347 0
eISBN 978 1 78450 681 0

Counselling People on the Autism Spectrum
A Practical Manual
Katherine Paxton and Irene A. Estay
ISBN 978 1 84310 552 7
ISBN 978 1 84985 473 3 (large print)
eISBN 978 1 84642 627 8

Autism Movement Therapy® Method
Waking up the Brain!
Joanne Lara with Keri Bowers
Foreword by Stephen M. Shore
ISBN 978 1 84905 728 8
eISBN 978 1 78450 173 0

THERAPEUTIC ADVENTURES with
AUTISTIC CHILDREN

Connecting through Movement, Play and Creativity

JONAS TORRANCE

Jessica Kingsley *Publishers*
London and Philadelphia

First published in 2018
by Jessica Kingsley Publishers
73 Collier Street
London N1 9BE, UK
and
400 Market Street, Suite 400
Philadelphia, PA 19106, USA

www.jkp.com

Library of Congress Cataloging in Publication Data
Names: Torrance, Jonas, author.
Title: Therapeutic adventures with autistic children : connecting through
   movement, play and creativity / Jonas Torrance.
Description: London ; Philadelphia : Jessica Kingsley Publishers, 2018. |
   Includes bibliographical references.
Identifiers: LCCN 2017059779 | ISBN 9781785924552
Subjects: LCSH: Autism in children--Treatment. | Autistic children--Treatment.
Classification: LCC RJ506.P66 T67 2013 | DDC 618.92/85882--dc23 LC record
available at https://lccn.loc.gov/2017059779

British Library Cataloguing in Publication Data
A CIP catalogue record for this book is available from the British Library

ISBN 978 1 78592 455 2
eISBN 978 1 78450 831 9

Printed and bound in Great Britain

In memory of Sheila Coates

Acknowledgements

I would like to extend my deepest gratitude to all of the remarkable friends, colleagues and parents who have helped to deepen my understanding of autism over many years.

This book was greatly helped along its way by Dr John Richer, Matt Trustman, John Torrance, Barbara Bender, Annie and Richard Brooks, Sam Settle, Rebecca Smart, Franco Scabbiolo, Penny Best, Kathy Erangey and, most of all, Kate Carne.

Finally, I am absolutely indebted to all of the children I have worked with, for showing me their light and allowing me to share it in this way.

Contents

Introduction

Autism

I first worked with an autistic person in a residential setting. It was the early 80s and 'Autism' was handwritten in his file. Unsure of what the term meant, I turned to a colleague, who gave me a remarkably simple explanation:

> If you go to an autistic school at playtime, you will see all the children playing outside. But they don't play with each other.

This introduced me to the first fundamental principle of autism: the 'separate-ness' or 'self-ness' of autistic children. Divided up into its component parts, the word 'autism' means auto-ism: the way of the self (Silberman, 2015, p.5).

Understanding the concept of 'separate-ness' is useful but also limited. Another aspect of autism, and one that many autism experts would agree upon, is that *autism defies definition*. For example, I know now that autistic children quite often do play with each other in the playground. Some love to be touched or enjoy loud music or even sudden change and socialising. Everything that you learn about an autistic individual will be tested by the next one you meet. Any person who is in a position of knowledge about autism (and that includes autistic people themselves) needs to recognise that we are individual human beings first and autistic beings second.

'Autism' first appeared in the first half of the 20th century, from the collective efforts of, amongst others, Grunya Sukhareva in Russia, Leo Kanner in the USA and Hans Asperger in Austria. Arguably, Leo Kanner first chose the word as a diagnosis. But all three noticed similar traits in the particular children that they were studying (Silberman, 2015, p.98). Sukhareva, Kanner and Asperger worked in a time when grand unifying theories were popular. They therefore looked for and found similarities in the children they studied. There was a steady gathering of data, theories and momentum through the rest of the 20th century, all reinforcing the ideas, concepts and diagnosis of autism. Autism became more recognised and diagnosis increased. When the initial diagnosis of autism could no longer support such an increase in usage, the diagnostic terms began to split apart: Asperger's syndrome, dyspraxia, obsessive compulsive disorder, high functioning, low functioning, attention deficit hyperactivity disorder, pathological demand avoidance, oppositional defiant disorder, spectrum disorders and many more. Rather than focusing on the similarities, diagnosticians began looking for differences that would allow them to use some of these other labels. Faced with so many labels, the recipients often became increasingly uncertain and confused.

Donna Williams simplified the whole issue by suggesting the image of a 'fruit salad' (Williams, 2006). She explained that autism is not one thing: it is a mixture of different dispositions and traits, which she described as 'fruits'. When some or all are placed in the same bowl (person), they can be collectively called 'a fruit salad' of autism. Each bowl is necessarily unique, with its own particular flavour.

When we look at individual variations in this way, we can start to uncover specialities, as well as specific human strengths and weaknesses. From these discoveries, we can genuinely begin to help each person to help himself or herself. There is not, and there should not be, a 'cure' for autism, but there are ways of making lives easier, more communicative and more joyful.

In this book, I have simply used the term 'autism' or 'autistic' throughout, except in Chapter 13, where the term 'Asperger's syndrome' (American Psychiatric Association, 1994) is at the heart of the story. Opinion varies about 'correct' terminology, and so in the absence of certainty I have gone with what appears to be at least a general consensus amongst those who actually have the diagnosis. With an admirable simplicity, autistic people themselves often prefer to be called exactly that. It's understandable that terms such as 'disorder' would fall from favour, but even the use of the words 'spectrum' and 'condition' can be seen as unnecessary embellishments. Autism is autism. Another bugbear that some have is the use of the word 'with', for example 'a person *with* autism'. Many autistic people have pointed out that autism is not an added component, or an 'app'. It is an integral part of their lives.

Telling stories

This book is, at its heart, stories about children. If you wish to read a book about theories of autism, therapy or development, there are many excellent ones to choose from, but this book is not intended to be theoretical. I know from my own experience as a therapist that people love stories and relate to them in a very different way from how they relate to theoretical information. One can talk to an autistic child about change and pathways and strategies, but if you tell them the story of another child, perhaps a little bit like them, it goes like an arrow, straight to the target.

The children who feature in these stories must be recognised for their generosity and courage. Most of them are adults now and each one (or in some cases their parents) have consented to their intimate tales of therapy being told. Some of those involved even asked if their own names could be used, but for consistency's sake, confidentiality has been protected by the use of pseudonyms. The details of their whereabouts, homes and settings have likewise been protected. Suffice to say, they are/were all autistic children from various places in the UK. One or two of the older or short stories are not individual people; they are 'composite' characters, changed in a number of ways so that they are completely beyond identification. Nevertheless, when you read the stories, you will recognise real people. You will recognise them in your own children, classes, therapy sessions and play schemes. Each story exemplifies a key aspect of autistic behaviour. For me, the children are the stars of this book.

This book features just two girls, and both of those stories are from a time when I was not working as a therapist. The reason for this is straightforward. As a therapist, I have mainly worked in a team, and in most cases it seemed appropriate for the female therapists in the team to work with the girls. Nevertheless, I have worked with many girls and still do. I have noticed, completely anecdotally, that autistic girls tend to be more private than the boys. Therefore, their stories have for the most part not been available to be published in this book.

Who is this book for?

If you are reading this book, you will probably have some curiosity about children with autism. If you are a parent, these stories may offer an insight into autistic children in general and also why your child behaves in particular ways. In addition, it will, I hope, give you the tools to approach the challenges that you face with increased confidence and creativity. Similarly, I hope that teachers and carers will gain fresh inspiration as well as practical ideas. For therapists, I have tried to highlight the intricacy of the autistic experience, and the need to meet that experience with flexibility and patience. Last but not least, autistic people themselves may find glimpses of their own childhoods in these stories. If this is the case, I hope that they are encouraged to tell their own stories in their own ways.

Therapy

Even though therapists are highly trained, have ethical guidelines and supervision and are committed to easing the suffering of the individuals whom they work with, it would be a mistake to imagine that only a qualified therapist can work in a therapeutic way. In fact, in order to offer the best help to an autistic child, everyone around that child – parents, teachers, friends and carers – need to awaken their therapeutic mind.

When qualified therapists come to work for the first time in the field of autism, they quickly realise that they have to unlearn and relearn significant parts of their otherwise useful training. Autism is more than a completely different world view, because autistic children and adults see, hear, feel, smell, taste and generally sense the world outside and inside themselves in sometimes radically different ways to non-autistic or 'neuro-typical' people. The therapists' usual training in and understanding of emotional recognition and regulation is, therefore, no more than a mark on an otherwise featureless map. As therapists, when we work with autism, we have to start from scratch.

This book honours the reality that autism is, despite our best efforts, still mainly uncharted territory. At times, in these stories, I am brutally honest about my lack of understanding or my misjudgements. Learning is a central part of therapy and I learn as much as my clients do. If things go well, there comes a point when both the child and I are learning together. This may seem like an odd approach, but to learn or play together is in itself a radical movement away from the stuck and solo operations of some autistic children. The therapy journey is uncharted territory for the child too and in many of the chapters, I am simply sharing the delight of a child who is discovering new ideas.

It's important to understand that therapy with autistic children takes time. Some of the stories in this book cover a therapeutic journey that lasts years. This is because it can take longer to establish a therapeutic relationship and also because a common feature of autism is stuckness. There are no absolutes of course; I have known significant change to take place in weeks or even in a one-off session. But in my experience, for most autistic children, therapy is not a quick fix.

Dance movement therapy

In the UK, we have an association of dance movement psychotherapists, of which I am a member. In America and Europe, the profession is known as dance movement therapy or DMT and, for simplicity's sake, I shall refer to it in this way in the book. Dance is of course as old as humanity, and its place in ritual and healing is well known (Chodorow, 1991). Recently, a boy told me that he 'hated dance'. I had known him for some months so he was surprised when I told him that I was a dance movement therapist (DMT). When I'm working with a child, their story takes precedence over everything else. He did not know that I was a DMT because it had not been necessary for me to mention or demonstrate it up to that moment. He had his own needs and agenda, and for me to encourage dance with him would have been, as the Zen masters say, 'like putting legs on a snake' (Carne, 2016, p.41): in other words, a pointless exercise. The young man in question was equally surprised, however, when I pointed out to him that in fact we had been dancing. His favourite activity with me was 'Chi Sau', the Chinese art of 'Sticky Hands' (Edwards, 2005), a martial arts form of interaction, where the partners rhythmically flow to and fro like a wave together. The partners attempt not to lose contact with their hands and arms as, at the same time, they try to unbalance each other. He agreed with me a little sheepishly that, yes, one certainly could call that dancing!

As I have explained, the key thing for any therapist to grasp about autism is the different view. This is what a DMT can bring to a therapy session. A DMT is always thinking about, and moving with, the body of their client. This is a fundamental and elemental way to work. For children with communication difficulties, it is, I would suggest, essential. The DMT's world view is one that sees and feels the interactional shaping of bodies (Best, 2003) and the weight and flow and the movement of the eyes and head. Flicking, dabbing, flapping and tapping (Bartenieff and Lewis, 1980, p.57) are recognised and incorporated into the communicative experience. Yes, a DMT works with words and mental constructions, but we also honour the presence and interactions of the body. Whether I am drawing, talking or playing with glove puppets, I am also trying to stay with the 'felt experience', that is, what the body senses. This primary sensory experience is not only known by autistic children in themselves; they often seem to recognise it in others too. They understand that you are, in the gut and the bones, with them.

The arts and creativity

I have had the good fortune to spend a lot of time working with other arts therapists: music, art, drama and play have all influenced my approach greatly, as this book demonstrates. Again, these approaches were not placed upon the children, and each child seems to require a different activity. It is endlessly fascinating to be with autistic children as they negotiate their way around a dance or painting or song. They rediscover themselves in the art form. Many autistic children who can speak report to me that they can't remember much from earlier times in their lives. The high velocity and sensitive tone of the autistic mind means that a lot gets left behind. When children engage in a creative art form, they begin to re-member themselves. They reconstruct their psychophysical body and become someone anew. Creative arts also give children an opportunity to imagine themselves as someone else. Those with challenging behaviours often become regarded in very set ways, because the people around them need to prepare for the problematic behaviour. This can mean that the children also get set in a mould of feeling that 'I am and always will be like this.' With this inadvertent reinforcement from the adults around them, the situation can grow into an enormous, stuck problem. Working creatively and therapeutically with the arts can offer a lifeline to all concerned. The children can reimagine themselves and, with help, a real change in behaviour may emerge.

Mindful approaches

Mindfulness is now used extensively in the treatment of a variety of mental health and chronic pain conditions. Its success is well researched and documented (Kabat-Zinn, 1990). The efficacy of meditation and mindfulness practices as therapeutic tools drew me to incorporate them into my work. But it is not always the most appropriate approach. Many of the autistic children I have worked with were uninterested, bored or actually quite worried by set mindfulness techniques. So, I let the children themselves decide what they enjoy and want to pursue. I have also recognised that a creative attitude is needed when teaching meditation to autistic children. Some of those whom I have worked with enjoy the stories and the history around meditation. The dynamic tales of great meditators inspire them to try simple techniques for themselves. I have also let go of my attitudes about doing meditation 'correctly'. Children, for example, who find relaxation almost impossible, can develop ways to concentrate for extended lengths of time on thoughts and objects. Others may have significant difficulties breathing gently or with the diaphragm. But they often report that the techniques still have a positive effect. Indeed, in quite a few cases, staff told me that they would arrange for the children to do particularly difficult pieces of work following their mindfulness therapy sessions, because at that time, they knew the children would be able to manage the work.

This could lead us to think that all autistic children might benefit from a creative and flexible approach to mindfulness. I believe that the approach is helpful for some, but real care and experience are still required when teaching mindfulness. When the teacher or therapist has an established and disciplined meditation practice themselves, the children will be able to 'believe' in them. Mindfulness needs to come from the heart. Mindfulness teachers need to naturally embody and demonstrate its benefits in their own everyday life and interactions.

A sense of purpose

I worked for many years in a pioneering setting. We were encouraged to use our initiative, and all reasonable ideas or approaches were attempted and evaluated. Over time I was able to experiment and as a result I gained a broad experience and, most of all, a huge respect for the young people I worked with. Nevertheless, working with autistic children can be tough. Progress can be slow and erratic and the families around the children can vary greatly in their abilities to cope. With children especially, we are all aware of the passage of time. Neuro-typical children develop at a clear pace, week by month by year. It can be frustrating and deeply worrying to watch, for example, an autistic teenager apparently miss out on a vital period of social development, because he or she is playing video games. From this frustration and worry, a large industry has grown up offering solutions to 'autistic problems'. This book also offers some solutions, but they are all embedded in the individual stories of the children. In most cases, with a bit of nudging, the children themselves discover their own ways through difficulty. Certainly, some basic attitudes and approaches do seem to have been more effective in this field, and in each chapter they are clearly explained. The strength of these therapeutic approaches is that they are set out not in a generalised strategy, but in each personalised story.

The approaches that are outlined in this book are mainly there because, first, the child in question liked and responded to them and, second, because I happened to have these particular skills. Because I practise martial arts, yoga and meditation, I tended to reach for these skills alongside my experience as a DMT. This book, therefore, is an invitation to go out and create your own stories and approaches. The reason why there are so many strategies and techniques for working with autism is simply because there are so many autistic people. Ultimately, it's not autism or strategies that win: it's people – children, like the ones in these chapters, their parents, teachers and friends. Out of many, we are one. So, please, read and enjoy. Then play, dance and draw yourselves and your children into new worlds of learning and adventure.

1

IN THE MOMENT
Stepping on Sunlight

David liked the school field; it was large and open. And whilst all of the other students were in class, it presented no social entanglements either. We walked and talked, circumnavigated this great feathery, green sea. When words ran out, we began to run, David slightly ahead, bouncing on the balls of his feet. The field was surrounded by trees, planted regularly around the perimeter. In the early summer they were all in leaf and, on this sunny day, they cut clear shadows on the green grass. The shadows were long in some places and short in others, and they had gaps between them. I don't know exactly how, but between us we devised a game of stepping only where there was shadow and avoiding the sunlit grass. The game gained excitement as we both ran faster, leaping and racing from shadow to shadow. David always found routes that carried us on and on without delay. He was happy because he could move freely from shadow to shadow. He enjoyed the feeling of being like water running downhill, finding a way, opportunistic and unstoppable.

We gradually made our way around the large field. The angle of the shadows changed and the shadows became shorter, but David still found a way, dashing on tiptoe along slithers of shade. Looking up ahead I could see a problem: the trees stopped abruptly about 30 metres from the end of the field. The shade and the game was running out. I said nothing, curious to see what David would do.

David continued, concentrating exclusively on the shadows at his feet. When he suddenly reached the great expanse of open, unshaded grass, he stopped dead.

David's mind was running on, bounding forward, but his body was motionless. I could see there was a struggle going on. He stood, unusually still, looking at the grass in front of him. He eventually lifted a foot and tentatively placed a toe onto the sunlit area of grass. He experimented with this, then, as he planted his foot down carefully. He murmured to himself, 'There's a shadow under my foot when I put it on the ground.'

David took a couple more tentative steps until he was surrounded by sunlight, then suddenly he turned and faced me. He was lit up by both the sun and some inner light of realisation. He smiled broadly and declared, 'I can step where there's shade and where there's sun. That means I can go anywhere!'

David turned and, yelping with delight, he raced off across the wide open expanse of the field.

2

UPSIDE-DOWN ELEVATOR RIDE

At five years old, Luke was new to primary school when I first met him. He had round eyes in the middle of a round face. His huge circular glasses goggled at people and toys, and were always on the move. On the top of his head was a buzz of feathery blond hair, which, with a firm, pouting mouth, tended to make him resemble a duckling. He had a pronounced lisp that didn't stop him chattering enthusiastically about his 'most favourite things EVER!'

Luke was also remarkably controlling, even by the standards of the other autistic children at the school. Toys were strictly lined up and moved in sequence, any formalised schoolwork was completely rejected and his diet was massively restricted to the couple of items that he allowed into his lunch box. Luke had a very engaged mother who was kind but also firm with him. She held the line, as did the staff at school, but still he would not give in to the many and varied demands of the school day. He *had* to be at the front of the queue. He often shot off in the wrong direction. He collapsed shrieking when asked to work and absolutely refused to go to the toilet, even though he was plainly desperate at times. It seemed that his cute, fluffy exterior was masking a toughened campaigner who was determined to win at all costs.

Chairs

We played in therapy and Luke loved it. He enjoyed immensely having an adult who joined him and followed his wishes. He was imaginative within his restricted frameworks and loved high-octane chasing and 'I always win' games. The problem was that, eventually, it had to end. He had a countdown towards the end of the session, but in some ways this made him worse. At first he tried desperately to construct the game in such a way that it was endless. Then he tried the 'just one more' technique, but when it became clear that I was stopping, he had what is in common parlance known as a 'meltdown'.

Anyone who has witnessed an autistic child in full 'I'm not having it' mode doesn't forget it. Luke's version of this well-worn pathway involved shrieking, slapping and charging around the room. His distress was genuine. Tears shot from his eyes in jets and his circular glasses became completely fogged up as, from the neck upwards, he went a deep salmon pink. He had also, at some point in his short life, acquired the technique of throwing chairs.

At first he threw one or two, but when he got no response from me, he threw every chair in the room. As luck would have it, we were in a disused classroom, and there were a lot of chairs. He was only little, so he wasn't heaving them across the room (although that would only be a matter of time if the behaviour wasn't addressed). He was actually quite artful with the chairs: he would flick them and spin them so that they crashed in specialised ways.

I decided to get interested in Luke's diversity of chair throwing. I commented on the way he turned and toppled them. He quickly caught on to this and started throwing to order, developing his style. As this continued, he became calmer and started to talk about what he was doing. At what seemed a hiatus, we managed to bring the session to an end and I was left with nothing worse than a pile of chairs to pick up.

I made sure I prepared carefully for future sessions. I arranged the timetable so he could stay a bit longer if need be and shifted some of the chairs out of the room. I still gave him a cue that the session was going to finish, but I didn't give him an anxiety-inducing countdown. I also shortened the length of our play period. The main focus became the ending, to the extent that at times the ending period became longer than the main session itself.

Gradually, we worked on two things: different ways of 'flipping' chairs and how to pick them up. We played a game where he had to flip them over as fast as he could whilst I had to try to pick them up.

The shift came one day when I flipped a chair. Luke was outraged; he said in his best parental voice, 'NO! You must *not* do that.' I said, 'I AM going to do it,' and immediately flipped another one. Before long, we were both laughing and racing around the room as he desperately tried to pick up chairs after me. From then on it was relatively easy to get Luke to help tidy up at the end of the session. Even when he was distracted or unhappy, he would still replace one or two.

I wondered where this chair game was going. Would we be stuck in an endless loop of chair flipping and replacing? To my surprise, one day Luke came to the room with an idea already in his mind. He lined up two rows of chairs in the middle of the room and asked me to me sit down. He then sat at the 'head' of the rows and suddenly we were on a bus! Once the dry kindling in his mind was lit, it quickly caught fire. In no time I was playing different characters getting on and off the bus, whilst he, the ever-patient driver, kept me exactly informed of the route and what adventures were in store.

The destination of the bus was always the same. The seaside resort of Burnham-On-Sea occupied an almost-mythical place in Luke's mind. His holidays there (he did not allow his family to go anywhere else) were internally catalogued. He had a 'mind map' of the whole seafront and he carefully introduced me to every attraction. But the attractions were not necessarily the same as those that the tourist board might specify. Luke was keen on the bus depot, the train station and the jewel in Burnham-on-Sea's crown: the elevator in the shopping centre. In the corner of the classroom was an empty walk-in cupboard. This became the Burnham-on-Sea elevator. Once we started to play in the elevator, the chairs were left behind. From that day on, Luke never flipped a chair in our sessions again.

Elevators

In Luke's imagination, we rode the elevator up and down the building. He worked an imaginary panel beside the door and we emerged out of the cupboard onto new floors and new surprises. I was curious about the possible new lands that the elevator might take us to, but Luke always wanted us to return promptly to the elevator. For him, it was the journey. We scaled the imaginary building, rising and falling through ever-increasing numbers of floors. It wasn't long before Luke's control panel became more sophisticated. He controlled the speed; often the elevator would crash and things began to take a more manic and wild turn. The elevator became 'The Crazy Upside-Down Lift', which sent us hurtling in darkness through all directions around the cupboard and landing in a heap on the floor. Sometimes Luke asked me to physically lift him off the ground and to spin and turn him upside down.

When we played in the elevator, I started to notice that Luke often hopped and twisted in the way that children (and adults) do when they need to go to the toilet. By now Luke was able to wee in a school toilet, and, as luck would have it, there was one right next to the classroom. But his movements and smells were suggesting a more significant event. Of course, I asked him if he wanted to go, but he grimly said no and sometimes bent double to try to hold it in. Unfortunately, the game he was so keen to play was not helping. As soon as we returned to the imaginary up and down of the elevator he found himself crippled with internal movement.

Eventually, I stopped him and said, 'Luke, I know you really need to have a poo. If you go and have one, I promise you that as soon as you are finished you'll feel much better and then we can carry on playing the game. I will wait for you.'

Luke seemed to be almost torn in half, but eventually he conceded. He insisted that I came with him and he was experiencing such pain and fear that I was required to talk through the door to him. He had quite a ritualised way of going to the toilet and I verbally had to take the place of his mum or dad, helping him get through it. On our return to the elevator, he was ecstatic with relief. Two barriers had been broken: the first, that he had gone to the toilet at school without his parents' help; the second, that his game was not irretrievably lost. The interruption was an inconvenience, but no more than that. The chain of events and thoughts had not been broken; we could restore the game.

From then on Luke tended to have a poo most weeks when he came to see me. Even at home it was a rare event and I often had to pass a message to Mum: 'Yes! He's been!'

Toast

As time went by, I began to think more about Luke's highly restrictive diet. There were two aspects to this problem. The first was that he only ate a couple of items at school: Peperami and crisps. This obviously was having an effect on his bowels and indeed his general well-being. The second problem was that he absolutely only ate food that came from home. He refused anything from the school site, such as biscuits made in cookery or birthday cakes sent in by other parents.

For someone who was so restrictive in terms of food, Luke enjoyed eating, and he particularly enjoyed playing with the *idea* of eating. One of our destinations in the elevator was an imaginary café. We set up tables and chairs and I served him whilst he ordered sumptuous imaginary meals, pretending to eat all manner of interesting foods. One week, I brought in a drink that I knew he liked and included that in the game. He was very pleased to pour it out and I joined him. He said happily, 'This is the best drink EVER!' as we both sat with plastic beakers. He watched me very carefully as, after saying 'cheers' several times, I drank. He put the cup to his lips, but the liquid no more than touched them.

We continued the game with no reference to the success or failure of the drink, but each week I started to bring more ingredients. I focused on drinks and toast with various spreads. Luke absolutely loved making toast and preparing a table; he even curtailed his beloved elevator games in order to play this new café game. Each week we worked together to prepare a meal as he chattered excitedly about the process. After some weeks of Luke paying close attention to me eating and drinking, I noticed that he was drinking small amounts himself. The toast was a bigger hurdle. He liked choosing different spreads and spreading them himself. He even held the toast up to his mouth saying, 'Mmm delicious toast!' Then, in the same way as the drink, slowly but surely, the toast started surreptitiously to go into his mouth and down.

From start to finish in this process, I ensured that I did not praise him. I stayed in character; we were two friends making and eating a meal. I made no comment at all about the amount he ate or didn't eat. I wanted him to feel completely at ease in the game with no pressure whatsoever. It was a kind of trick...in plain sight.

In time, toast and Marmite became a staple for Luke at lunch-times. When the other children got their lunch boxes, he went to the kitchen and made himself toast. Once the barrier was broken, he was able to sample other foods available in the school. He still remained faddy about food, but with a lot of work from his mum and the teachers, his diet was able to broaden out from the beginnings of our 'café'.

POSTSCRIPT

Dreams

I continued to work with Luke throughout primary school. At 11 years old, he moved to secondary school and I felt it would be good for him to move on from therapy at the same time. Over the next couple of years, I still continued to see Luke in passing, and the news was good. He was doing well, attending classes, learning and making friends.

When Luke was 13, I received a message from his mother: was there any chance I could give them some advice about difficulties at home? I arranged a visit after school and on the chosen day I travelled to their house. Luke, his younger sister and his mother all sat with me in the living room. I noticed that Mum's usually cheerful countenance was looking drawn. She admitted straight away to being very tired. 'It's Luke,' she said, 'he's still getting up in the middle of the night (around 4 am) and he gets into bed with us. I try to get him back to his room, but if he's had a bad dream he won't go and it keeps us all awake.'

Luke drew his feet up onto the sofa and curled his now long body into a comfortable position. He began to recount his dreams. They were dark, fearsome tales that involved being chased and eaten by faceless mouths with needle-sharp teeth. Unlike most children, Luke didn't wake up when he was caught. He had to endure the experience of being eaten alive by the monsters before he was able to jolt himself awake.

It became clear to us all that Luke wasn't getting into his parents' bed for entertainment. He was desperate for sanctuary from his own mind in the long, dark hours of night. We sat and talked about the dreams, the details and what they might mean. We brought them into the light. We also talked about the dreams that other family members had, helping Luke to recognise that nightmares were not unique to him. We all share bad dreams. We also talked about good dreams – fun and exciting events that you can't wait to get to sleep for.

The next day I received a message from Mum, saying, with some relief, that Luke had slept through the night.

REFLECTIONS ON LUKE

There is a trinity of early developmental milestones for children. This comprises eating, toileting and sleeping. All three are essential for life and, like breathing, they can all be controlled to some extent, but only at a serious cost to the child's health. An autistic child often has an extra layer of resistance and anxiety when it comes to these milestones, and there is evidence of this in Luke's story. First, let's have a closer look at eating.

Eating

Luke had learned the mechanics of eating fairly easily. He had some simple tool use and could find his mouth and chew without great difficulty. The problem was more around Luke's attitude to eating. Over his short life he had quickly built up a very careful system about what and when to eat. Coming to school had immediately pushed this into the light. Although you won't find 'eating' on any school's curriculum, food and its consumption may require special attention, especially for young children.

Luke was, in essence, frightened about what was going into his body. When Frances Tustin coined the term 'the autistic shell' (Tustin, 1990), she was talking about a kind of protective psychological shell that autistic children may create around themselves in order to feel safe. This is why autistic children often appear 'alone'. They are protecting themselves from the unclear and unpredictable world of other people by keeping their distance. They may not want to be alone or separated out; it is something that they do out of necessity. It's akin to a survival instinct.

In the same way, Luke was trying to protect his physical body from the external 'invasion' of food. An autistic child wants to be complete, whole, without any external influence. In our interactive world, this quickly becomes a problem. Social situations and timetables can be negotiated. But we all have to eat.

Theoretically at least, Luke wanted to eat. He was interested in food and showed great curiosity in our café game. He loved it, because he could play with the idea of food when it was outside his body. When a child plays with an idea, they *are* taking it in, or 'ingesting' it, but they are doing so with their minds, rather than physically. This, for Luke, was quite enough for some time. 1 at no point encouraged or discouraged him from eating. We simply played a game. As part of the game *I* ate and drank. This is known as 'modelling'. 1 was showing Luke how to do it, giving him a pathway and permission. The rest was left up to Luke's natural senses of hunger, development and curiosity. He made his own choices, and when a child is able to do that, there's generally no looking back once they start down their chosen pathway.

When the idea of eating in school was desensitised by his experiences in therapy, Luke was able to bring these new possibilities into the wider school. He was cautious, but the school gave him the independence of making his own toast. He ate with the others and learned to chat and have fun at lunchtimes. He was wary about brought-in food, but at times he decided to join his friends in trying an occasional slice of birthday cake.

Toileting

Autistic children sometimes experience severe problems around urination, but the powerful physical, tactile and sensory experience of excreting faeces is very particular and links strongly to the themes of 'inside the body' and 'outside the body', which we have already encountered through Luke's eating issues.

Usually poo is associated in a child's mind with being something unpleasant. It's smelly, nobody seems to like it and it's completely removed as soon as possible. This presents a particular conundrum for a child, because the poo has come directly from them and it therefore follows that there is something bad inside them that is trying to get out. When we combine this with Tustin's theory of a protective shell in autistic children, we can see why Luke might be determined to keep the poo inside himself. If we then add newer theories about fragmentation and autism (Richer and Coates, 2001), it becomes possible to see that autistic children who have an uncertain view of their disconnected and fragmented body would, at all costs, try to hold themselves together. They do not want to flush part of themselves down the roaring toilet.

Luke was interested in elevators for a variety of reasons. But one simple, physical fact was clear: when he and I repeatedly played at going up and down in the elevator, it seems to have simultaneously suggested to Luke's bowel the muscular up and down movement of the anal sphincter known as 'peristalsis' (Yeo *et al.*, 1955). He had subconsciously hit on a game that was physically and psychologically encouraging him to poo.

For Luke, there was also a worry about time. When he was in the middle of something, he didn't want the activity to be interrupted or 'cut short' by an unwelcome trip to the toilet. He was anxious that he would never be able to return to where he was in the activity and that he would, in essence, lose himself. As we can see in Luke's story, he needed a lot of reassurance around this. I had to rearrange the schedule of our sessions to accommodate Luke's difficulty with endings. In the same way, I also ensured that we had time to return to our play after Luke had been through his extended toilet break. It can be difficult to arrange sessions flexibly with children, especially in school settings. But there are times when they desperately need the reassurance of completing a task and knowing that they can return to where they were. Then they can become whole again.

This theme of going the extra mile with autistic children also informed me when I accompanied Luke to the toilet. If at that crucial point I had said, 'I don't do that,' or gone to get a different member of staff, the moment would have been missed. Either Luke would have managed to retain the contents of his bowel or there would have been an unpleasant mess. A therapist needs to be able to move easily between the psychological and the practical, and respond wholeheartedly to whatever is happening. At this moment, Luke needed help in the toilet and I was able to provide it by supporting him from outside the cubicle.

Sleep

Most autistic children suffer from problems with sleep. There are various specific medical conditions connected to sleep and hyperactivity (Richardson and Friedman, 2007) but Luke, in this story, illustrates a very common issue that is once again connected to the theme of inside and outside.

For Luke, the difficulty is with a bad dream that is inside the mind. If a child is worried about having a nightmare, they may put off bedtime because bedtime means sleep, which in turn means the nightmare. Sometimes autistic children become especially focused on video games at night. This in itself is, of course, a problem. Playing lively games and staring at a light source (a computer screen or TV) does not aid sleep, but it may be that the child is trying to build up their mental activity specifically to prevent themselves from sleeping and dreaming. Quite often, autistic children, if they are able, will tell you of a fierce focus on a game or activity at night until a point when they virtually pass out. Sleep, when it comes, forces them into submission. As a result, some of these children have no experience of how to relax gradually and succumb gently to sleep. The whole bedtime experience for them tends to be stressful.

Luke gets to bed in the end, but once he wakes with a bad dream he cannot cope with being on his own. In the middle of the night, he will only say that he had a bad dream. He is probably scared that talking about the dream will somehow bring it back, or even into reality, so he keeps his nightmare locked up inside. As a result, it keeps returning when he sleeps. Because Luke has had therapy, he understands the use of speaking his inside stories. He just needs to reconnect in order to bring his dream out into the light and share it. He will have more nightmares, of course, but now he has a way to bring them out. In the mind, in the night and on your own, dreams can be consuming and terrifying. When we share them in the daytime they are less powerful. We can begin to make some sense of them and understand how they are a useful part of our being and our lives.

Child development does not go in a straight line. We don't learn to look, walk and talk in a straightforward order. Early developmental markers, such as eating, toileting and sleeping, overlap and inform each other. Luke's story shows us how there are strong themes that underlie this process, even in very young children. Luke found it hard to understand and accept that his internal view of the world would have to adjust to a different external reality. This difficulty displayed itself through his cautious developmental progress in eating, excreting and sleeping. So, when we come across a child who is 'developmentally delayed', we need to examine their stories around the delay as well as the practicalities of helping them from milestone to milestone. When we work with the whole of the problem in a creative and practical way, we give the child the best opportunity to move forward holistically.

Children have a powerful force that urges them to develop. If there is an impasse in their development, this force to progress developmentally doesn't go away but builds up in sometimes unhelpful ways. Luke was stuck, but not static; he was putting a lot of energy into organising his world and imposing his will on others around him. Rather than push against that energy by saying 'no' to his compulsions, I joined him in an exploration of his world. As he relaxed into our companionship, so things started to emerge – literally, in the case of his bowel. His own internal developmental force was pushing him towards joining in, becoming a part of things and growing up.

PRACTICAL POSSIBILITIES

1. If there is a difficulty with eating, remove pressure by using imaginary play around eating, shopping, cooking and communal dining.

2. To play with, or encourage, the idea of bowel movements, use substances such as play dough wrapped in plastic or cling film to encourage a child to squeeze and squash and twist the dough in and out of the plastic wrapping.

3. Encourage the whole family to talk about their dreams in the mornings, good or bad. Have a whiteboard or paper to hand so that the children can draw what they see in their dreams.

3

'TEACH ME TO MEDITATE'

Rowan did everything in quick time. He moved, without hesitation, straight to the centre of a situation. He was certainly able to think, but in the moment he was all action, all hands and eyes, rushing towards often dangerous and disruptive dilemmas.

Once, without warning, when a member of staff was searching for something in a cupboard, Rowan leaped to the cupboard door and slammed it shut with the member of staff inside. In the next instant he locked the door, rushed to a window and threw the key far away into a hedge in the garden next door to the school. Another member of staff and I were there at the time and neither of us was able to stop him. His movements were so sudden, particular and directed that we did not even manage to lay a hand on him before the key went sailing out of the window towards who knows where.

After he had thrown the key, Rowan seemed absolutely calm and was even willing to help free the member of staff. He came with me quite happily to ask the neighbours if we could search their flower bed, and after a while he found the key and helped release the slightly traumatised staff member from her dark prison.

At home, his behaviours were often harder to deal with. He regularly and without warning attacked family members, who became battered and bruised by his assaults. Sometimes he set fires and had also broken several TV screens.

Rowan was slender, with sharp eyes and a rapid, gravelly voice. He would occasionally twitch his face or bark a sudden word. He had a diagnosis of autism and Tourette's syndrome (*DSM-IV*, American Psychiatric Association, 1994). He was both funny and rebellious. From an early age, he used to scrawl his name on any surface. He drew a circle around the 'A' in his name, creating the anarchy sign long before he really knew what it meant, but anarchic was what he was. His speeded-up and chaotic internal life collided with everyone else's slower and more ordered external one.

Playing with hyperactivity

Using a behaviour modification approach with a boy like Rowan was pretty much useless. He understood the function of sanction and reward, but didn't understand why these things should be outside of his control. Also, in the moment of a sudden storm of actions, Rowan was completely unable to think and therefore couldn't use thinking processes to stop himself from doing something. He required a different approach: that is to say, an approach that had intimate meaning for *him*. I therefore decided to try imaginative play with Rowan.

For the next year and a half, we met every week in school and played together. Rowan's games were exciting and adventurous. Danger seemed always close by, and we both suffered a lot at the hands of various anime and Pokémon-style characters, but we generally emerged victorious. To be the winner or to be 'on top' was vital for Rowan. For him, the world collapsed if he lost. By playing, he could work through these battles and vanities without anyone getting hurt. The play was his; I was simply a partner or witness. It was very physical, with lots of running, crashing, chasing, escaping and so on, but the power for both of us was in the shared landscape we created and moved around. In this world, Rowan could be fast, dangerous and impulsive. At times, this approach was difficult, as the play became *too* physical and there was a possibility of someone getting hurt. At those times, we'd have to stop, take a reality check or ease off for a while. However, at the end of each session, Rowan quickly returned to the truth of who he was and who I was. We'd often talk through issues of school or home whilst making our way back to his classroom.

As Rowan moved towards being a teenager, his behaviour eased a little at school, but he remained unpredictable. He went through a period where he became withdrawn, and one day when I arrived at school, the staff told me that he had locked not someone else but himself in a room.

I went to the room in question and, after talking with Rowan through the door, he allowed me in, quickly locking the door behind us once I had entered. The room was transformed. He had moved furniture out of the way and created a large space in the middle. He had also gone around to every window and door and carefully shut out any external light using black paper and tape. The fluorescent tubes inside the room were off and we were in a kind of half-light. He had created a sensory cave for himself in this room. Sound and light were reduced; the stimulations of objects were cleared away. I later learned that he had done something similar at home in the attic. The purpose of this cave was twofold. On the one hand, it was a calm and completely controlled environment for him; on the other, it also meant that he had withdrawn himself from all the people in school.

Learning meditation

Rowan sat down, cross legged, opposite me on the floor. For a whilst he was silent, then he asked, 'Can you teach me to meditate?'

It was unusual for Rowan to ask for something in this way. He tended to either take something or wait until a particular activity was offered. It was clear to me that this was something he had been thinking about. Indeed, he explained to me that he had attempted meditation himself in his attic at home. I realised that the sensory cave had yet another purpose: it was his attempt to create an environment that was conducive to meditation.

I asked Rowan why he wanted to learn to meditate and he told me he wanted to gain powers. He talked about Japanese-style superheroes and samurai and how they became empowered through meditation. He was particularly interested in being able to control things, for example, to move and levitate objects.

Although this is not a useful motivation for learning to meditate, it is quite common. One way or another we want to feel empowered or in control. We want to feel that we have a foothold in a sea of confusion. Rowan was no different, he just happened to be caught up in a glorious fantasy of control.

Most importantly, Rowan was sincere in his wish to learn something from another person. For most of his time at school he had avoided learning anything much from anyone, so I told Rowan that initially he would have to learn ways to quieten his mind and that I could help him with that.

On that first day, I showed Rowan four different types of meditation: sitting, walking, standing and lying. In each position, I emphasised focusing the mind on the breath and I taught him a couple of simple techniques, such as counting his exhalations, to help him do this. Rowan was very diligent; he carefully followed everything that I showed him. He had a very strong will to learn, and he seemed really driven. Although I explained as clearly as I could that he should count silently, he chose to count his exhalations out loud. He also did not initially understand that he only needed to count his exhalations to ten, and then repeat. Instead, he counted out loud up to 60. I let him do this, as I could see it helped him focus and it was demonstrating his desire to do the practice.

He found sitting crossed legged on the floor difficult, so I showed him alternatives like sitting in a chair. However, Rowan seemed to need the difficulty of the 'classical' posture, and so he persevered with it. If he chose to suffer a bit, that felt acceptable. He had made others suffer in the past and somehow now he was trying to do something wholeheartedly helpful.

I was pleasantly surprised when, the next week, Rowan wanted to continue. From that day on, our previous schedule changed permanently. Every week we would practise various forms of meditation. He quickly realised that the whole purpose of meditation is simply about observing the mind. He also realised how hard this is and was happy to put levitation on the back-burner. After a while, he also became interested in martial arts, and we gradually developed a programme of traditional Kung Fu forms, seated meditation and relaxation techniques. Of course, we went through ups and downs. Some days Rowan appeared very twitchy and distracted. At those times, he opted for 'deep pressure', which involved me pushing down with my hands on Rowan's back, legs and arms, whilst he lay on the floor, breathing in and out.

Over time, and partly through watching movies, Rowan developed a deep interest in the elements and how they could be interpreted through martial-arts-style movements. With his imagination engaged, he was now in receive mode. He asked me to show him different styles of Tai Chi and also found diagrams on the internet that we carefully worked through together. He never lost his practice of seated meditation. He found sitting still extremely difficult, but when I told his mother one day that he had managed to sit still for nearly half an hour, she simply couldn't believe it. She had never seen him stationary for more than a couple of minutes at a time except when he was asleep.

When Rowan left school around a year later at 16, he was a much-loved character in his specialist setting. The other students respected him and enjoyed his still-mischievous company, whilst the staff found him kind, funny and manageable. Before he left, Rowan secreted messages all over the building for future students, encouraging them and assuring them that the staff were good people who could help them. He was emotional when we parted, and we both agreed how grateful we were to have met each other.

POSTSCRIPT

I lost touch with Rowan for some time after this, but I knew that he had gone to a residential school to continue his studies and give his family a much-needed break. One day I was visiting another boy at the residential school in question. As I left, I suddenly heard my name being shouted out. I turned and saw a slim figure in the window before he ducked out of sight. It was Rowan, and he asked the staff at the school if he could see me. The next time I came, the two of us sat for a while in a lounge and talked. He explained that he wanted to show me the grounds of the school, where he played with the other pupils. We went out with a member of staff (because the school rules dictated that a visitor shouldn't be left alone with a student). Rowan took us to an area of woodland and led us to a copse where several young trees had been bent over and down, held into a sculptured shape by other trees and undergrowth. Rowan explained that he and his friends shaped the saplings in this way every break time, creating undulating shapes through the wood. The staff member with us assented that this was true. 'I don't know why they do it,' she murmured.

With his piercing black eyes, Rowan looked at me and asked, 'What do you think?' I took a moment and placed my hand on the soft, smooth bark of the tree. I said, 'Well, they are young rowan trees. Like you; you are a young Rowan. As you are training yourself, you are also training the trees, shaping them. You've held them down, but you've made lovely shapes with them, so they're beautiful amongst the other trees.'

Rowan gave a broad smile. 'That's it,' he said. 'That's right.'

REFLECTIONS ON ROWAN

Meditation and the human condition

Meditation as an approach can be useful in many ways. But before any big claims are made towards developing yet another method or strategy that can help autistic children, we need to recognise that mindfulness and meditation are understood to be helpful interventions for people in general. Rowan did not show an interest in meditation because he's autistic. He showed an interest because he's a human being and was naturally drawn to ancient and beautiful practices such as meditation.

This highlights a crucial point: *we are human first and autistic second.*

With all the attention and interest on the unusual and special nature of autism, it can be easy to forget that we all have far more in common than we have differences. It is actually quite easy for non-autistic or 'neuro-typical' people to recognise and empathise with the excitement, sensitivity, confusion and anxiety that autistic people experience, because these are universal human conditions. It's just that in the autistic experience, they are extreme. If you'd like a shorthand way to describe autism, then it's just like living as any other human being, but amplified...times ten.

Bearing this in mind, it's useful to be cautious about universal strategies for autistic children. Rowan found meditation a useful method for self-help at a certain time of his life, but just as with any part of the population, other autistic people may not.

The fulcrum of this story was the moment when Rowan made an active choice to investigate meditation. Up to then, he was having things done *to* him by lots of well-meaning people, myself included. This is the situation that parents, teachers and autistic children find themselves in most of the time. The child is either not doing enough of something or doing too much, or they are doing the wrong thing. So, adults have to intervene and steer, cajole and pull the child in more constructive directions.

There always comes a point when any child will have the desire to try something new and something potentially constructive. With autistic children, this moment can be rare and fleeting, so we have to pay very close attention to the child, looking for clues, waiting for any sign of a 'sea change'. When that shift comes, we need to act to create as much support as possible around the child. We must not *steal* the new idea from the child, perhaps to make it 'better' or more worthwhile. For the child to own the idea is everything. This is how change happens, by constructive movement and ownership, from within.

Rowan certainly made others suffer – he was violent and unpredictable – but he was also suffering himself. When children behave in ways that are upsetting, they sometimes distort large parts of their character to justify to themselves why they are distressing others. Parents and teachers may get the impression that autistic children either don't care or actively enjoy being violent. There are times when this can be the case, but what is usually happening is that the autistic children have successfully created a convincing persona. Not only have they convinced others, but also they may have convinced themselves that they are 'bad' people.

All this personality change and justification required relentless attention from Rowan. Add to that the sensory confusion of autism and the uncontrollable and compulsive actions of Tourette's syndrome, and you have the ingredients for a highly stressful life. Rowan was initially attracted to meditation through fantasy martial arts/video-game characters. He was impressed by their power, but underneath this he also recognised their self-control, their ability to cope and stay calm.

Being calm is a fundamental tool for any therapist, especially when working with hyperactive and anxious children. Sometimes this is not given the importance it deserves. Richard Maguire talks about how autistic children and adults 'sense' people when they meet them (Maguire, 2012). An autistic person uses their differently wired system to focus on how a person moves, smells and sounds. This information for them is central, and the sensory map that they make of a person often decides for them if that individual is

'OK' or not. If we are calm with autistic children, they notice, and they appreciate it. In time, they may also wonder how we got to be so calm.

Meditation is about settling into our true self. When we focus on the breath and let our minds quieten the usual chatter, we feel different. We feel secure and at ease. To do this, there are a variety of methods. As described, with Rowan, we tried sitting, walking and lying-down techniques. Rowan in some ways wore his mind as a suit of clothes. In other words, he physically did whatever he was thinking. Many of us have probably fantasised about locking someone in a room, but at the time when it was possible we did not act, we just *thought* about it. Rowan *did* his thoughts, as it were, in real time. This meant that Rowan needed a physical, doing approach to calming the mind. He found it hard to be physically still because his mind was escaping into his body and moving. For this reason, he liked to sit on the floor, cross legged with his hands placed together. This position locked his body somewhat: it physically focused him. It is well known that autistic children and adults seek ways to 'hold' the body, often using props such as stretchy blankets, weighted jackets and even Temple Grandin's famous cattle crush (Grandin, 2009). Sitting in a formal meditation position is simply an ancient way of doing the same thing.

At other times, when Rowan was particularly stressed, he chose a lying-down relaxation technique. In this case, the body is 'held' by the floor, with constant sensory feedback. It sometimes took a long time for him to be still. At these times, we would bring awareness to the mental processes by following the breath or focusing the mind on simple themes. Eventually, usually after about 20 minutes, his body became more still as it harmonised with his mind. Even on especially difficult days, when it seemed to me that Rowan couldn't become still or focused, he reported an improvement. Sometimes I could see it, sometimes I could not, but he was changing.

Receptive and directive approaches

Rowan's story also highlights a central theme in parenting and development: the question of when to allow the child and when to say no. In Taoist philosophy, these are known as the 'receptive' and 'directive' attributes (Lao Tsu, 1972).

A receptive parent is the kind of parent who is *alongside* the child. She creates a helpful learning environment for the child and lets them explore it with few boundaries. She is curious and interested in what the child does and lets the child find his or her own pathways for learning and development.

On the other hand, a directive parent is one who structures the environment for her child. She creates boundaries and leads the child to the most helpful places for learning. The directive parent will intervene and make a judgement on behalf of the child about what is and is not the right way to go.

Neither parent in these two models is wholly correct or incorrect. Neither loves her children more or less and both of them are equally trying to help their children as best they can, each from a different viewpoint. Of course, in reality all parents have aspects of both the receptive and directive in the way that they interact with their children. But we all generally tend naturally to lean one way or the other.

It is common for autistic children not to like being told 'no'. Rowan, for example, had a very strong reaction to being told 'no' or having his chosen pathways restricted. This would suggest that the receptive approach is a good place to start with him. Certainly, trying to control very adverse and contrary children is, at the very least, extremely hard work and ratchets up potential conflict. A frequent comment from parents about home life is, 'It's like living in a war zone!'

So, let's all just be very nice and easy and unreactive and unrestrictive with autistic children, right? It's easy to see there's a 'but' coming, and the 'but' is, of course, how will that go with everybody else they meet in everyday life? In fact, we need to recognise that if we start with a receptive approach with a child, we naturally need to be heading, in due course, towards a more directive approach. If, on the other hand, we find that the best way forward with a young child is to be quite controlling and directive, then, in time, we need to work towards relinquishing that control and taking a more receptive stance.

Rowan was, within himself, very directive, but unfortunately his direction was erratic and unhelpful. He was erratic partly because he may have actually been trying to correct himself, but in doing so, he went wrong again, and so on. His direction was unhelpful because sometimes his actions were out of his control. This chaos brought out a strongly negative and anarchic alter ego, which was again directive – forcing situations and being reactive.

By the time Rowan made his decision to take up meditation, he was ready for a receptive approach – to just be with himself, drop judgements and not react to everything around him. Over time, he became more relaxed and gradually that trickled out in his interactions with others. As he became more at home with himself, so his directive nature was able to find its place too. There is no doubt that Rowan realised, correctly, that he had to actively control himself, but he needed the receptive side of his nature to do this effectively. In the Postscript section, earlier in this chapter, he gives us a graphic example of how he changed his external environment to demonstrate his internal being. But it's likely that a younger Rowan would have simply broken the saplings. The older Rowan was more in touch with his receptive nature and recognised that the saplings needed to be *steered.* He learned to control the power of nature by shaping it. He used the growth and flexibility in the saplings to create a garden.

PRACTICAL POSSIBILITIES

1. When playing with a child, take note of any areas of interest in the child's play, which may be suitable for more formal learning. Tip off the child's teacher to see if he or she is able to bring these areas of interest into their lesson time.

2. Children who retreat into a sensory cave may need to do so, but may also become stuck in their cave. Join them inside, if they will allow you. Otherwise, sit at the entrance and share with them your view from outside the cave.

3. Autistic children tend not to see the symbolic side of what they do. Suggesting an additional meaning to their play and activities can be useful when it is done subtly.

4

THROUGH THE SWINGING DOOR OF AUTISM

This next story comes from more than 30 years ago, when I was just starting out on my career. Within living memory, autistic adults and children were locked up and kept away from general society. In fact, there are still parts of the world where this is commonplace (Murray, 2008, p.17). The reasons that are usually given for this are either to protect society or to protect the autistic people themselves. Either way, when we are working towards being more enlightened about how autistic people can be part of society, we need to recognise that there is a history of discrimination towards autism. Although society has moved on, autistic people still often experience a lack of understanding from those they encounter.

Sarah

Sarah came from a secure place, a hospital. She and several others were being moved out of their lifelong home on a ward, as the hospital in question was being closed down. The motivation behind the move to small group homes was founded in positive new ideas about care for learning disabilities. But the move was also inevitably and inextricably tied up with economics: the change was being allowed to happen because it would save money.

When Sarah arrived, she came with the clothes that she stood up in and some underwear in a small battered suitcase. There was also a worn toothbrush, a flannel and a pair of slippers. At the age of 19, Sarah appeared to own no personal items at all: no wristwatch, jewellery, posters, books – nothing. Then in the bottom of the suitcase I found a small piece of metal that looked a bit like a hairgrip. On closer inspection, I saw that it was a mouth harp. This is a metal toy instrument that makes a variable twanging sound when you hold it to your lips. When Sarah saw it in my hand she snatched it away, placed it in her mouth and, with a careful look of concentration, paced around the room rhythmically twanging the mouth harp.

Sarah was only 19, but she had been sent to live in a home with adults, as she 'made up the numbers' and came from the same hospital as they did. She was tall and slender, with hair the colour and consistency of straw. I discovered later that she was not at all keen about either a comb or a hairbrush. She had pale-blue, wide-spaced eyes and an angular, boyish face. She spent a lot of her time on her feet, pacing and scampering, often flapping her hands and flicking her fingers. She made only a few verbal sounds: 'mmm' and 'oooh' when she was happy. When she was not happy, she had a piercing and long-lasting shriek. At those times she ran hard and fast, often slapping her head as if simultaneously chasing out an internal enemy. She was an escapologist and on more than one occasion she was found wandering the roads of the local area. She probably perfected her techniques in a locked ward, so a group home in the community presented no problem for her. She paid close attention to combination locks, timers on doors and so on. When she wished, she could find a way out.

Sarah was separated from others her own age in her ward at the hospital. She had no visible family. She tended to keep her distance, avoiding physical touch. She did not speak or give eye contact. I had never met anyone before who was so completely alone.

At that time, I was roughly the same age as Sarah and designated as her 'key worker'. The group home was newly built and a bit of a flagship for the area. It was agreed that new staff needed full training. So, my colleagues and I were carefully trained to cut nails by a chiropodist, brush teeth by a dentist and deliver enemas by a nurse. We received no training at all in learning disabilities, mental health or autism.

I recall that we had a staff meeting where our co-ordinator ran through the residents with us. She had some reports and had met nurses on their wards. When she got to Sarah, she summed her up by saying, 'If you gave her five pence, she'd most likely swallow it.'

Learning on the job

To say I was unprepared for the work is an understatement. Luckily, I'd worked previously in a training centre for adults with learning disabilities. It was far from perfect, but it had been a happy and vibrant place, so I had some understanding of what other young people like Sarah could be like and I recognised that she was falling far short of her potential.

Armed with skills in chiropody and cleaning, our staff team set about trying to improve Sarah's life through the medium of personal hygiene. We bought her new clothes and tried various ways to keep her clean and presentable. Sarah varied in her responses from resistance to bemusement. She had no idea what we were doing or why. We weren't aware that she needed to have an explanation. We simply assumed that this was good for her and was therefore what she wanted. We were basically kind to her, however. We spoke in pleasant voices and tried to include her, so over time Sarah snatched at food and tried to escape less.

Sarah had absolutely no input from any therapist or indeed teacher. At 19 she was seen as beyond school age and she also had a description of 'uneducable' written by a doctor in her file. She was destined to a life of non-verbal communication with no alternatives on offer. We, the staff, had no training, time or resources to offer Sarah. Nevertheless, everyday life threw up opportunities. Sarah had bodily responses to what was said to her, moving away or towards depending on the offer. Some staff used this as a kind of game. They interpreted her interest in objects or activities as affection for particular staff and her moving away as dislike for others. It was patronisingly primitive compared with the subtle ways that Sarah could read keypads and double locks, but at least it put her at the centre of attention. At last, after seeming almost to not exist, she started to 'take up space' in the home.

Sharing music

One day Sarah became upset. Her charging around and screaming was in turn distressing the other residents, so I managed to steer her into a side room. Once inside, Sarah flung herself onto the couch and bounced up and down. The frame of the couch was creaking under the weight of Sarah's body as it bounced up off the cushions

and then came crashing down again. But my main concern was
the noise. In the small room her wailing and shouting was like a
physical assault. Ordinarily, we might well have left her to it, but
something about her distress made me stay. Should any human
being have to suffer like this? And what on earth could I offer to
help anyway? I was faced with the starkness of Sarah's situation.
She was like a beacon on the high seas, sending out a clear distress
signal, but she seemed to have no way of receiving any message of
empathy or relief. She was alone and lost in her turmoil, and my
desperate wish to help outweighed, for me, the physical discomfort
of the noise.

I took hold of the only object to hand: the mouth harp. Sarah
often wandered up and down the landing twanging away on it;
perhaps, I thought, it might soothe her. I put it to my lips and
started to play. It turned out that it's difficult to play anything very
soothing on a mouth harp. It's an entirely rhythmic instrument,
with only short tones. Anyway, the sound did not pacify Sarah.
She continued to bounce vigorously on the couch. I did notice
that her verbal noise decreased a bit; it was as though she wanted
to hear the mouth harp and needed to make less noise to do so.
I started to twang the instrument in time with her movement as
a sort of accompaniment to her. She varied her movement, her
hands came up and she began to flap wildly as her head rapidly
twisted from side to side. The feeling of connection to her through
the accompaniment on the mouth harp made me continue. I no
longer felt I was trying to change her state. I was just being with it,
recognising it.

As the seconds turned to minutes, Sarah became quieter;
she was still moving her head and hands frantically, but she was
listening intently to the sound. It seemed to be filling her being,
and she led my playing with her intricate movements, fingers,
eyes and mouth. She was dancing.

It was hard to keep up with her musically. I had only twanged
a mouth harp a couple of times before and now I was locked in a
performance. The movement of her hands and head became faster
and faster; saliva rolled down my chin as I tried to keep up. This
was hard work! Harder than cooking or cleaning.

Finally, Sarah started to smile broadly, grinning, showing her
teeth. From deep down inside her, a chuckle rose up and blossomed

into a delighted, gurgling laugh. I had never heard her laugh before. I was so shocked that I stopped playing the mouth harp. She looked straight at me for just a second. In that moment, I felt I saw her whole story. I saw sadness, but also the richness of her inner life, her unique view and, most of all, her absolutely indomitable spirit.

The seconds passed. Sarah, now silent, jumped off the couch and upright in a single bound. She avoided my eyes and deftly plucked the mouth harp from my hand. She walked straight out of the room with no sign of any change other than the fact that she was now calm. I stood for a moment, unable to fathom exactly what had happened. It was my introduction to the 'swinging door' of autistic interaction. The moment of deep connection was gone, the door swung shut, and I had no way of knowing what was now on the other side of the door or when it might swing open again.

REFLECTIONS ON SARAH

This story takes place long before I had received any therapy training. It's also from a less enlightened time. But it does demonstrate a fact that was true then and is still true now. Most of the therapy that takes place with autistic people is not done by therapists. Instead, therapy is, knowingly or not, facilitated in the main by parents, care workers, teaching assistants, siblings and other (autistic) peers. Working as a care worker, you get long hours of contact and this leads to a trust and intimacy that most 'one-hour-a-week' specialists could only hope for. A parent or care worker is much more likely to be there when life events happen. When the 'swinging door' opens, they are the witnesses.

The witness position

In dance movement therapy there is a specific role or placement that is described as 'the witness position' (Adler, 1999, p.143). This means the ability to be on the outside of the event and have a wider view. We could compare it to a camera in the corner of the room, but we are not cameras. Human beings have an interactive quality whenever we are present in a situation. The witness position is found when a person sees the whole picture and has a degree of impartiality, whilst at the same time recognising the part that they, the witness, plays in the whole scene. The witness position sees, but is also seen. This is particularly important for autistic children, many of whom do not like to be watched. They sometimes have a powerful sensory reaction to 'sharp, hard eyes'. So, in these situations, an observer needs to practise a particularly gentle witness position. They can develop a softness of gaze and use peripheral vision more, moving the eyes slowly around, rather than a long, hard, silent stare.

The witness position is helpful for autistic children because it puts them in a soft spotlight. It presents an opportunity for the child to imagine how they may appear, without being told. Because this is such a difficult and central issue in autism, autistic children usually pretty quickly get tired of being told how they seem to others. Words can be punishing in these situations. Quiet observation, without strong focus, can create an arena in which the child can start to question and even look at themselves.

Sarah had been organised and told what to do her entire life. At some undefined point in her childhood, events and people had come together to decide that she would never be able to organise herself. So, she was placed and maintained in a hospital. It's obviously tragic that Sarah had not been nurtured and was thwarted at every turn when she stole food or tried to explore. Her view was not considered; her voice was not heard. She was not in any way seen as anything more than somebody for whom and to whom things are done. I described her as a ghost. A lot of the time she was like that: not there. It was only when she was disruptive that some sense of self emerged and could be seen. This is how important challenging behaviour is. Her 'naughtiness' was pretty much all she had left in terms of an identity. When we meet someone like this, it's vital that we don't smother and negate their behaviour. Their behaviour is their voice and we have to listen. We need to occupy that wider, witness position. When we do this, the challenge will always eventually subside. In Sarah's case, she simply became tired of launching herself up and down on the couch. Because I stayed, I was then in the best position to witness what emerged out from the difficulty and the behaviour.

Going through

Another advantage that parents and care staff have with autistic children is that they *go through* problems. They are there at the outset, they go through the crisis, and one way or another they are there when the dust settles. Very often they are also there when it starts all over again!

Going through issues is closely linked to autistic difficulties with transitions. When autistic children struggle to cope with a change of events, it is very similar to the difficulties that they may have, for example, with going through a doorway into a new room. When events change, autistic children are shocked by the change and don't want to accept it. They literally want to turn the clock back; they don't want the event to have happened; they don't want to have the finality of going through *that door.* Autistic children can and do stop themselves from going through doorways, but they cannot stop everyday events: somebody *did* shout, there *is* a new Doctor Who, etc. This means that children can be forced into a feeling of non-reality, which makes them either retreat into themselves or strike out in anger and distress.

In Sarah's new home, something had happened that caused her distress. She couldn't cope with the event so she screamed and ran about. Let's bear in mind that at this moment Sarah had in her life been given very little control over herself and the events around her. This made the problem worse, in that her usual resources (other people) were not fixing it and she felt completely unable to fix it herself. She was not even able to communicate the problem. So, there she was: once again alone, on the high seas with her irreparable difficulty. At no point did I know or even attempt to solve the initial problem that had made Sarah upset in the first place. Metaphorically speaking, I had passed with her through the doorway of the previous difficulty, and was there with her screaming and facing the new problem: Sarah's behaviour. So, Sarah may have still been in the past event, but I was with her in the present moment. When, as supporters, we scrabble around and try to fix the past problem (for example, to talk about the old Doctor Who), we may distract the child, but we are not doing her any favours. We have to go through, so that the child feels emboldened to do so as well.

Changing channels

A mouth harp was all there was to hand that day, but, in fact, if I had whipped out a cello whilst with Sarah and tried to counteract her hyperactive distress by playing soothing music, I may well have added to the difficulty. Sarah and I engaged in something known as 'changing channels' (Mindell, 1985). That is, we changed the channel from bouncing distress to fast music. Arnold Mindell calls it changing channels because he likens the experience to watching a TV. We stay with the TV, but we shift the channel, changing from thought to emotion to image to sound and so on.

We can change channels in many ways, for example, bouncing a ball in time with a person's movements or using colours or lines in painting to show something about how a person is speaking. Changing channels works particularly well with people who have unusual sensory experiences. If people 'smell' colours or 'see' sounds, they very naturally respond to changing channels. The benefit of this technique is that it shifts the focus for the child. It takes away the immediate pressure of, say, screaming and changes it into, for example, a *looong*, drawn-out movement, such as sliding hands across a table. Very often when autistic children are upset, they can't find a way to change their experience. Changing channels values how they feel, whilst offering some relief. The relief can bring a space, even momentarily, which in turn invites them to find, and feel a little more comfortable in or with, a witness position.

Sarah and I stayed with the rhythmic quality of the moment but we shifted away from distress and pain. The emotions started to blend into the music and the dance. This was us 'going through' the doorway together. I saw very clearly when Sarah came through her doorway how transformative this experience can be. I also saw that these moments contain golden opportunities for communication. Sarah was only able to hold my gaze for a moment, but someone who is non-verbal is usually very skilled at the forms of communication that they do have. She was able to tell me in that brief moment that she was prepared to meet and trust me. The doorway only stayed open for a very short time, because Sarah's habitual way of being drew her back into herself almost immediately. But at least I was left with something to remember, as well as a deeper insight into how to connect with Sarah.

PRACTICAL POSSIBILITIES

1. Only hold onto distressed autistic children if they want you to do so, or if it is a last resort and in order to keep them from harm. Steer a distressed child towards prepared, quieter environments. If possible, avoid stairs if you are moving with a physically erratic person.

2. Use soft sounds and a quiet voice to direct a child. Avoid the word 'no.' There is no need to verbally empathise. Staying with the child is reassurance enough. If you have to leave the room, make sure you can still see and hear the child and that they can interact with you if they need to.

3. For those that have issues with doors, create a door and gateway project. Make models of Japanese-style 'Torii gates' or get them to use old keys that open and close boxes. Create games and models for children to practise going through doorways in a variety of ways.

5

INTO THE WOODS

Sandy had mousy hair and bright-blue eyes. His face wore an intense expression that spelled determination and 'don't get in my way' in equal measure. He was compact and muscular and moved like a dart – quickly, taking the most direct route. His eyes looked straight ahead as he searched for the next thing to investigate or to dismantle. He was not a large boy, but he seemed to take up a lot of space. In response to Sandy's sharpened body language, people around him tended to keep their distance, as this was generally the safest approach for all concerned.

School

Whilst still at primary school, Sandy broke another child's nose with one straight punch. Of course, he also did a lot of other things at that school; for example, he read every non-fiction book in the library and corrected teachers who embellished their lessons with anything that was not exactly true. He even had some friends. But, unfortunately, what everyone most remembered was the fact that he broke another child's nose.

Out of necessity, Sandy entered a more specialist provision. Gradually, his reputation for violence grew, and he often had to be tutored in a room that was separate from other children. In the room, the staff erected a tiny pop-up tent, which became Sandy's den. He retreated there after 'blow ups' and did not need to hang a 'Do Not Disturb' sign outside: his Alsatian-like growling was enough to keep people away. The teaching assistant who took him into some mainstream lessons was usually a nervous wreck afterwards. She once described to me the sensory hell of the main corridor at break times. She could set Sandy on his course, but, as other pupils entered the corridor, there would inevitably be physical contact, which in Sandy's eyes meant starting a fight. She and other members of staff, including another therapist, valiantly tried to keep him educated, but it was hard enough work trying to keep him in school.

Finally, when he was 13 years old, the time came for Sandy to move to a large secondary school. His father predicted that, even with extensive support, he wouldn't last two weeks. In his third week, Sandy busted out in some style. A combination of an annoying pupil and a science experiment gone wrong led to Sandy throwing a fire extinguisher across a large crowded room, upturning a science table covered in equipment and then fighting a running battle with teaching staff in the school yard. Sandy, as always, managed to find weapons, in this case a large metal pole and a chain taken from a nearby skip. Amazingly, no one was seriously hurt, but once again Sandy was out, banished from the school site.

A new place, a new chance

At this point, a rather unusual setting was found for Sandy. A small cottage next to a woodland nature reserve was already in use for a small group of older students, who in one way or another didn't quite fit in. They were all diagnosed as autistic, mostly with a clearly defined learning disability. Sandy was the most able in terms of speech and understanding, but this didn't seem to bother him; in fact, it seemed almost immediately that a pressure had been taken off him. The setting was quiet and homely. The staff concentrated mainly on practical tasks, and when they did do schoolwork, it tended to be seated at the large kitchen table, with the smell of baking cookies filling the air.

Every week in the cottage, the students spent a whole morning doing chores: cleaning the house and so on. Sandy applied himself happily to this; he especially liked to fix things, or at least take them apart – putting them back together again never engaged him quite so much. There was a large secluded garden around the cottage where Sandy had free rein, and on the occasions when he was not compliant or was unhappy, he would head out to a corner of the garden and thrash about. When he was left alone in this way, and with enough space around him, he became far less aggressive towards others.

I was already working at the cottage, and I had the idea that Sandy and some of the other students might find a tailor-made martial arts class useful. I set up a class that was facilitated by myself and a fearsome Kung Fu teacher. His brilliantly simple method was to teach these autistic students in the same way as he would anyone else. He respected them as both human beings and students of martial arts. The thinking behind this class was that Sandy in particular needed to confront something in himself. He needed to recognise who he was and what he did to other people. I had begun to realise that his ferocious and lonesome reputation had meant that he wasn't getting true feedback from others. In a physical sense, he did not know what effect he was having on others because they tended (quite rightly) to keep him at arm's length.

All the students loved the martial arts class. The teacher was so moved by their enthusiasm and willingness that from then on he particularly encouraged children and adults with special needs to attend his public classes. During our specialist classes, Sandy, for the first time, was able to glimpse the physical impact that he was having on others when he pushed, hit and kicked.

These were the beginnings of change in him, but another obstacle became clear: how could Sandy return from this safe environment of the cottage and specialised classes to the hurly-burly of formal education? He still had massive sensory issues with noise, lights and crowded environments. There was also a great deal of antagonism at home, especially with his brother. It was clear that more work needed to be done, so I decided that Sandy and I would to go into the woods.

Into the woods

Every week, Sandy and I turned left at the cottage gate and followed a trail, up past outbuildings, across an open grassy meadow, down a lane and finally up into a deep, wide woodland. Initially, the cover was mostly hazel; then it opened out into larger trees, oak, beech and silver birch. In the winter, sound travelled amongst the quiet trees, bouncing from crisp leaf underfoot to bare branches overhead. We caught glimpses of deer, wary even at a distance, and squirrels scooting along the branches above us. In the summer, once we stepped in, we were immersed, lost and completely alone under a muffled, green canopy.

I asked Sandy to go wherever he wished, but with the purpose of finding a special place, a place where he felt whole and at ease. Sandy pursued this task with great interest: he led me along animal trails, pausing and reflecting in different spots before moving on. We found a few places that seemed to be useful for us to work in, but soon Sandy found himself returning, week after week, to the same spot: a broken oak trunk beside a path in a small clearing, with ash saplings growing up around. This special place became our setting.

The setting held us both. One of the primary functions of a therapist is to be a 'container' (McMahon, 1992, p.10); that is, to hold the client's emotions and story, so that he or she is free to process and move through and on. But I was humbled and amazed by the ability of the woods as a whole, and this place in particular, to contain us both. Whatever happened there, whatever damage was done to the plants around us, when we returned the following week, there it all was – trees, earth and sky – waiting, with no judgement, ready to hold us once again.

With Sandy, a direct approach was necessary. I told him that we would be working with anger, violence and rage. I also told him that after every session I would drive him home myself and then sit with him and his father and mother, so that if Sandy felt unhappy or uneasy about anything that had happened, he could say, there and then. I knew and respected the fact that for once this 'dangerous boy' was now in a vulnerable position. He was far away from any help, in the woods with a man who wanted to work with violence! Sandy turned out to be a remarkably brave and perceptive boy. He took me at my word and trusted me. Right from the start, he knew he wanted to change and was prepared to face this difficult and unusual way of working in order to do it.

One of the first things I asked Sandy to do was to stand about five metres away from me and pick up a stick. He found a decent-sized one, and I asked him to throw it, 'towards me but be sure that it doesn't hit me'. I was expecting a missile to whizz by close to me, but, to my surprise, Sandy turned around in the opposite direction and threw the stick away into a bush. I asked Sandy to pick up another stick. 'This time,' I said, 'throw it closer to me; see how close you can get it without actually hitting me.' This stick came flying, with no hesitation, straight at my head! Luckily, I was able to duck and wasn't knocked out. After berating myself for being so stupid, I realised that at least I had learned something very important about Sandy. He was an all-or-nothing person: the stick either hits me or it doesn't. He had no variation of approach. I started to realise why he had got into so many fights.

Another time, Sandy was explaining to me how strong he felt. Indeed, he was strong, but more to the point, he was reckless, and this recklessness came from believing that he could do anything. He would smash through a window when another, more prudent child might think again because they were afraid of being hurt. Sandy had a very high pain threshold. He virtually didn't feel pain in his limbs at all. Many years later, as an adult, he took a knock on the hand and went to the hospital to get an X-ray. When they showed it to him, it turned out that every single bone in his hand had, unbeknownst to him, been broken at some time or another in his life. Sandy had a similar relationship with emotions. Like the broken bones, he knew that they were there, but found it very hard to feel them.

This relationship to physical and emotional pain tended to shape Sandy into a rather indomitable character. He felt he was invincible, a dark superhero of great strength. I was curious about the practicality of this, and I pointed to a young ash tree of about 20 centimetres in diameter. I asked him if he could chop it down. 'I could with an axe,' he replied. 'What about with a stick?' 'Sure,' he responded and set about finding a strong-enough stick. Once he was satisfied he had found a suitable weapon, he laid into the poor tree with an unbridled enthusiasm. When the tree showed only signs of external wear, he began to get more determined and even more angry. He thrashed and thrashed at it. Finally, he had to admit that he couldn't cut it down, but he quickly adjusted to the idea that he could *push* it down. Once again, he set to, possibly causing one of the many breaks in his hand. I had never seen a child so determined. He became more and more enraged until it seemed as if he might spontaneously combust.

Eventually, I asked him to pause. He was breathing heavily, his red face contorted into a snarl. I couldn't resist a classic therapist's question: 'How do you feel?' Ever the scientist, he paused and considered; eventually his reply was 'Hot.' Even at such a state of high arousal, he was only able to identify the most basic of bodily sensations. He seemed, at that moment, unable to access his emotional body.

I deliberately chose a young, thin tree because I knew it had the one thing that Sandy lacked: flexibility. No matter what he did, the tree bounced back with natural equanimity. He learned a lot from that tree; it was his match and he learned he was not unstoppable. He toyed with the idea that if he just had enough time he *could* break the tree in two. But as the weeks turned into months, it became a thing of amusement. I'd casually comment, 'That tree's still there,' and he'd smile wryly. Eventually, it became a symbol of the strength and permanence of nature for him. He looked at the wounds he'd inflicted on it and marvelled at how they healed, leaving no trace.

A lot of the work that we did together for the next two years was about the variation of tone that might be possible on the way to becoming violent or angry. With a lot of careful preparation, Sandy would allow himself to become *a bit* angry. Specifically, we worked a lot on 'stop' mechanisms. These were ways in which Sandy could remind himself to stop or turn or just shout instead of hit. We both recognised that, for Sandy, there was a point of no return, a point where he was fully clothed in aggressive defence and would act accordingly. The key was to work with the points of irritation and confusion before that. In terms of arousal, Sandy went from 0 to 60 in 0.0001 seconds, so our work was to increase that time gap, to give him an opportunity in real time to save himself, as well as others.

The stop mechanisms that we devised were not necessarily verbal or cognitive. We worked with the body. We studied the changes that took place in his body when he became aroused and we used them as markers. All the time, we tried to stretch the experience of anger, so that he bought himself time and, with it, the possibility of pausing, thinking and change.

Sometimes, Sandy would become detached and hard to reach, but he could still respond to my voice and to the great woods around him. On one occasion, he started to walk through the trees in a trance-like state. I was worried for him, but I knew that he couldn't be interrupted. Instead, I followed him at a distance. As he walked, I noticed that he was tapping and brushing against the trees. After a while, I started to create a similar music with my body as I moved. Then I sang: very simple forest noises of birds and branches but with a human voice, as I felt that he needed to know I was still there with him. He thrashed at things occasionally but kept moving. Sandy seemed to be working out a pattern of being upset without being engulfed or overwhelmed or lost. Eventually he reached the very edge of the forest. He stood on a rise, looking out from the dark forest interior to the light on the fields stretching out to a lake in the distance. I realised that his home lay in that direction.

I came closer to him and slowly, with one word dropping singly and quietly after another, we began to speak. Gradually, words came back to him: he returned to himself. I told him that we should leave, as a lot of time had passed. He looked at me and instinctively I walked away from him, leading the way, tapping and singing as I went. I didn't once look behind me, but I knew he was there by the sound of his own forest music.

Sandy often found it hard to put into words what happened in the woods when he arrived home. He needed privacy and his parents respected that. On this day, I said to his father, 'Sandy had a tough time today in the woods...but I think he's all right now.'

Looking at Sandy, his father just nodded.

POSTSCRIPT

Sandy, with a lot of work and help from those around him, managed to get and keep a placement in a residential college when he turned 16. He had various further adventures there, but at last he was able to get some academic qualifications and become a successful student in an educational institution. I met him again some years later at a martial arts class; he still trains with his original teacher and is working towards a black belt. He is also fully qualified in his chosen line of work and has a degree in astrophysics with the Open University. He very kindly accompanies me occasionally when I facilitate parents' courses, and talks openly about his past and present struggles and all that he has learned and achieved. In a short half-hour, he gives the parents more hope than I could in all the other weeks of the course combined.

REFLECTIONS ON SANDY

At a talk about children and autism, I once heard a well-known speaker say: 'Autistic children are *not* aggressive.'

At the time, I wondered to myself what this particular person would have made of Sandy. It was clear what the speaker was trying to say: that we should not confuse aggression with the sometimes challenging, sensory defence that autistic children use in order to cope with our loud and spiky social world. This is a very important adjustment that 'neuro-typical' people should be able to make when we consider an autistic child or adult. However, it is equally important to respect the right of any human being to his or her own emotions. Aggression is a highly powerful and fundamental human emotional state. To refuse autistic children their aggression is to somehow lessen their potential and experience of life.

Sandy was born into a highly particular sensory world. Light, sound, taste and – most of all – people were incredibly hard for him to process. And even when he was able to process them, he usually had to start all over again the next time he encountered them. The school bell and the school teacher were both extreme and sometimes unbearable experiences that required continual learning and relearning.

Sometimes, 'sensory' becomes a buzzword that is given to both explain and manage everything to do with autism. Having some kind of sensory map of an autistic child is indeed vital, and understanding how the filters in an autistic person's body/mind influence their view of the world and themselves is the absolute starting point for understanding autism. But it doesn't stop there. There is a reason why the word 'feel' refers to both the sensation of touch and the sensation of emotion. Our emotions, thoughts and actions constantly fold in and out of our sensory perceptions. So, when Sandy said (after fighting nature in the slender shape of a tree) that he felt 'hot', he was, in a very real sense, speaking from the heart.

Being brave

Anyone working with autistic children and adults needs to be brave enough to discard assumptions and cognitive baggage. Things are not always as they seem, for their client or for themselves. Is it sensible to teach a violent person martial arts? On the face of it, no. But in reality, it became a lifeline of support and training for Sandy, which he continues to enjoy and utilise to this day. Is it wise or safe to encourage a very volatile young man to become aggressive and enact his anger in the middle of a forest? Even now, I would not generally advise a therapist to do that, but the situation was desperate. Sandy was clearly an intelligent young man who was moving rapidly towards the educational scrapheap, not to mention potential violence with his family or the public and therefore the police.

The Tibetan Buddhist teacher Chogyam Trungpa said:

> You are a warrior when you have the bravery to face who you are, without fear, embarrassment, or denial. (Trungpa, 2009)

For Sandy, the key point is that he had to face himself before any genuine hope of change could happen. Sandy experienced a phenomenon that is not uncommon. That is, he completely forgot what happened during a violent incident. It was akin to a 'white-out'. At best, he could remember before and after and perhaps the odd flash of an image during the incident, but nothing more. This meant that he had very little to go on when it came to reflection and repair. It was as though it had happened to someone else. He couldn't own his actions, and therefore he couldn't change them.

The only way for him to work with his disconnect was through physical experience. The key was to create as safe an environment as possible in order to hold the anger. Sandy already used the outdoors as a way of escaping from himself, so we chose together to use the woodlands as an environment for facing himself. The fact that the woods were so large and quiet meant that the sensory influence was reduced and he could therefore feel spacious and free there. I made sure that everything we did was carefully planned. I didn't spring any surprises on him, and he always had the opportunity to stop by using a signal. We often repeated exercises and ideas as we worked on his issues week by week. He was a scientist and appreciated this methodical approach to such a volatile subject. We sometimes referred to our shared space in the woods as 'the lab': a place of experiment, of careful trial and error. This outside space was our laboratory, but there was also one inside. He was starting to investigate himself.

Will

Our work together was only possible because Sandy himself owned the process. This was at times a very confrontational and painful experience for him. It would be downright unethical to put a young adult in this situation without his and his family's consent. Ultimately, Sandy made it happen by one essential fact: he wanted to do it. He wanted change. He had the *will* to move forward and away from this chaotic existence. Ultimately, this is the most important factor in therapy with autistic children. Does the child want to change? Obviously, we encounter all variations on a spectrum of will. But a strong, firm desire needs to be either already present or sought out. Otherwise, the therapeutic intervention will be nothing more than window dressing.

Exactly where Sandy's strength of will came from is hard to say. His family certainly were determined and stuck by him at all costs. He also had resolute support from a variety of school staff and therapists. But most of all, it was in Sandy's being. His aggression, which had caused so many problems for him, became his catalyst for change. His aggression drove him forward and kept him determined. His aggression also gave me the permission I needed to go to the unusual lengths that such an extreme problem requires. Sandy demonstrated that autistic children certainly *can be* aggressive, but what we need to remember is that this aggression is simply a form of energy. With insight, patience and a bit of courage, this energy can help to produce a profound transformation.

PRACTICAL POSSIBILITIES

1. If an autistic child would like to join a martial arts class, arrange with the teacher for you to go along first and watch. This means you will be able to prompt the child with any problems that he or she might encounter (for example, shouting or physical

contact). Do not expect the class to adjust massively to the needs of an autistic child. The child needs to be ready to adjust to the rigour of the class.

2. Many autistic children feel claustrophobic in schools. When going to a new school, it is a good idea to introduce them to the school field or copse (if there is one). Also, arrange with them that if they suddenly have to leave the class, they will go to a predetermined place and you can meet them there.

3. If children find the hustle and bustle of school too disturbing, explore the possibilities of learning onsite after school, when it is quieter.

6

OK COMPUTER?

When I first met James, he was 12 years old. He was loose-limbed and had a broad, open face. His large head was framed by thick, dark hair. He talked a lot and focused heavily on his 'islands of interest'. When his subjects corresponded with those of other children, things generally went fine. But he found it very hard to deviate or be interested in other people's ideas. At times, his peers got bored and annoyed with his predictable, repetitive speeches.

The modern world of technology, specifically computers and video games, is a huge area of interest for autistic children. I had met many techno-obsessed young people in my time, but James seemed, even by these standards, remarkable. I knew from previous experience that to help a video-game- or computer-obsessed child, it's important to tackle the issue head on. Often, children would be desperate to talk about the games that they played, so my general technique was to let them. It was the 'long way round', and at times it could be mind-numbingly boring, but usually by the end of an hour I found that the child seemed at ease with me and was keen to come back to see me again. For my part, I had learned something about them. It was akin to panning for gold. I had to sift through a huge amount of drab, unimportant mud in order to find a tiny, shining nugget of truth about the child and why they were so interested in the game in the first place.

I took this same tack with James. In our first session, after he was a bit tentative about his clear *love* of computers, I said to him, 'You can talk to me about computers as much as you want. I'm interested and I won't stop you.'

It was as if someone had opened a sluice. The words poured from James: his computer loves and hates, his detailed knowledge of 'Super Mario' and 'The Legend of Zelda' and an overarching and profound admiration for all things Nintendo. Still the words kept coming. I didn't even have the verbal space to say 'mmm', as therapists are inclined to do! James leapt verbally from technological subject to subject. He recited whole pages of obscure technical data that he had memorised from the web. His voice was not slowing at all; if anything it was getting faster and faster. Then, abruptly, he stopped.

I looked at James. He had paused mid-sentence and seemed to be struggling. Suddenly, his face went a deathly grey and he keeled over to one side in his chair. I leapt forward from my own seat to stop him falling to the ground and at the same time instinctively said: 'BREATHE.'

Immediately, James gave a great inhalation, righted himself and within a few seconds was breathing normally. It dawned on me that James had been talking so fast and so urgently that he had forgotten to breathe. His obsession had overridden the body's most basic reflex. I took this moment to assure James that I would be back next week, so he didn't need to tell me everything today. We had plenty of time.

For the next few weeks, things followed a similar pattern, but thankfully without James passing out. Each session he greeted me enthusiastically and picked up where he had left off. James had a huge amount of data to verbalise to me, but even so, he tended to return to themes. Within the continent of his interest in technology, he had certain regions that he particularly liked to explore. One of these was the 'Virtual Boy'.

The Virtual Boy

The Virtual Boy was a hugely innovative and hugely hopeless game console that was launched by Nintendo in 1995. It was discontinued just a few months later, despite major publicity and financial backing. The Virtual Boy was a first attempt at '3D gaming', but back in the 90s, in order to make it 3D, the game was totally impractical and came with serious health concerns for users (GamePro, 1995).

James explained all this to me in great detail. Many years on (the console was created a few years before he was born), the devices were rare. James didn't have one, but he knew all about them. He spent a lot of time explaining the health issues connected with the console. Players were advised to use it for no more than ten minutes at a time because the red images and changeable parameters caused dizziness, nausea and headaches (GamePro, 1995). James told me that he reckoned he might be able to manage half an hour on one. He was fascinated by the contrast between innovation and failure. He desperately wanted the 'Virtual Boy' to be a success and railed against the powers that be for not seeing it at least as a first brave step towards the future of virtual-reality gaming.

It became clearer to me that James was not necessarily as deeply into video games as he was into the equipment that screened them. He was more of a 'hardware' than a 'software' enthusiast. In fact, as time went by, I started to realise that in some ways James identified himself as a computer. His outrage at the public trashing of the Virtual Boy came from a deep feeling that computers were sentient beings. James was struggling to relate to the human world, but he could imagine himself as a computer. It was therefore a little while until James finally started wondering out loud if I was as fascinated as he was by technology. It was a tricky moment. James was so fragile that he could shatter if he once again found a person who was uninterested in computers (and therefore himself). I told James that I wasn't necessarily that interested in computers, but I was interested in *him*. And if *he* was interested in computers, then I was interested too, because it helped me to understand him. At the same time, I made a mental note that we needed to find a larger room for our sessions. Our current room only housed a couple of chairs and a table. For James to be able to cope with a change in view, we needed to work in a different way. James was very stuck in his mind, so we needed to move his body.

Movement and the body

Our next room was much larger. It was an empty classroom on an upper floor with no chairs or tables. At first, James was rather lost. He stood stranded in the middle of the room with his head on one side, looking like a juvenile owl trying to understand the new space. After a while, we found various movement games that he enjoyed, which tended to be simple hiding-and-chasing games. James was ungainly in his movements – his arms and legs tended to fly off at unpredictable angles – but he liked to run around laughing and competing.

To help James integrate control of his limbs, we used Lycra sheets and bands. He liked to lie on the floor and be bound and wound up in the stretchy materials. At times, it looked too tight to me, but he enjoyed the strong feedback from the cloth. He was reminded of a loved teaching assistant at his primary school who used to pull him around on the hall floor in a cloth to calm him. He implored me to do the same. Several years and pounds later from primary school, this was a harder task. He would happily have had me drag him around the room all day, but I had to limit this activity each week, as it was exhausting.

Once James felt confident, I also started introducing deep pressure and body alignment as methods of integration and relaxation.

Deep-pressure work

'Deep pressure' is a concept that has grown out of research and investigation into sensory hyposensitivity in individuals with autism (Bogdashina, 2016, p.196). Hyposensitivity is essentially the opposite of the 'classical' view of autism. In other words, autistic children generally used to be depicted as being on their tiptoes, covering their ears and shielding their eyes. These kinds of children were over- or *hyper*sensitive to their surroundings and were trying to minimise their sensory contact with light, sound and touch. The problem was that not all autistic people fitted this model; in fact, some seemed to be completely the opposite. They stuck their ears against speakers, sat happily on hot radiators and gazed at the sun. These people, it was decided, were under- or *hypo*sensitive. They needed extra sensory feedback from the world around them in order to feel whole and calm. Pretty soon, on the back of that, it was recognised that actually a lot of autistic people have both hyper- and hyposensitivities. Depending on the circumstances, both are relevant for them. Like autism itself, sensory sensitivity is a spectrum, and autistic children locate their needs for stimulation or dampening down at various places on that spectrum.

Deep pressure focuses on a physical and psychological need to feel integrated in the body. It is not a particularly defined practice, but in James's sessions we used gravity and body weight. James lay on the floor on his front and I applied pressure to his outer arms and legs. Then, as James breathed in, I placed my hands on his upper, middle and lower back. As he exhaled, I gently pressed down, helping the air leave his lungs and giving him a strong sense of being on and held by the floor. We did the same with James lying on his back, but without the pressure on the chest cavity or stomach. He also responded well to gentle holding and pressure on his skull, especially at the back of the head and temples.

These techniques are not exactly prescribed in a manual. Often, parents and staff come across them by accident. A typical example is children who actively enjoy being squeezed in hugs or under cushions. Care is obviously needed with these approaches. They are entirely dependent on the preferences of the individual, and it is helpful and safest to have a good working understanding of anatomy, safe physical positioning and body movement.

Body alignment

Body alignment is rather more straightforward. In my work, I had started to recognise that autistic children tended to hold their bodies in various misaligned positions. Perhaps the head might be cocked to one side, or one shoulder was higher than the other. Sometimes the hips had a permanent twist as they moved. When the children were lying down, I started to correct their posture, lining up their legs, hips, arms and heads so that they lay in a smooth, clear line. I was surprised myself at the reaction; almost immediately the children became calmer and happier. This was the same for James. He seemed uneasy when he first lay down on the floor, but, before we tried any deep-pressure techniques, I lined up his limbs and torso, easing each arm and leg out with circular movements and a little shake. I spent time looking down his body and making sure that his spine was relaxed and in a natural line. Straight away, James became calm and stopped talking. By the time I finished the techniques at his head, he was often asleep.

Stickman drawings

I was interested in activating James's creative processes, so we started to draw together on a large sheet of paper. We took it in turns to draw a simple cartoon strip. At first, James was a bit bemused. His pictures were basic and didn't especially interact with mine. After a while though, James managed to get the hang of it and started to use 'stickmen' as his characters. He got the idea, like everything, from the internet, but quickly a simple narrative developed.

James had an invincible stickman called Steve and it became my stickman's sole desire to defeat or destroy Steve. James chuckled his way through increasingly impossible escapes for Steve. James's favourite method of thwarting my stickman was by simply negating whatever I did. So, for example, if I drew a shark to consume Steve, James simply drew an arrow pointing at Steve with a label saying 'shark proof'. Whatever I drew – a bomb, a gun, a spaceship – James virtually doubled up with laughter as he drew a small arrow and wrote a '----- proof' antidote. He particularly enjoyed it when I became 'angry' because Steve blatantly flaunted the rules of our drawing-game universe. I tried more and more outlandish and surreal ways to get Steve, but James always ensured that his character escaped and I would be foiled. There was a slapstick element to this story. James enjoyed the extremity of things going hopelessly wrong, with no hope of redemption. He was relentless in the way that he shut down any hope for my character, but his playfulness made it bearable. Through this play on paper, James was converting some of the destructive negativity that he experienced.

Generally, there was a good deal of destruction in the game. Both our characters produced more and more powerful bombs. The explosive power that we used became so great that, in the end, we resorted to showing our planet and indeed galaxy exploding from the viewpoint of a very distant planet inhabited by aliens who would comment laconically on the destructiveness of stickmen, saying, 'Those crazy humans are at it again.' James balanced this with a lighter planet, which he named 'The Party Planet'. There, everything was non-stop fun, balloons and excitement. Every now and then, James liked to return to this planet and just enjoy the sense of a fun, non-stop party going on in some corner of this universe.

WAKE UP!

One day, when we were sitting in front of our sheet of paper, James was talking about something he had seen on the internet. It was a piece of text that had become firmly lodged in his mind. James kept repeating the sentences, verbally turning them over. I suggested that we write the sentences down:

> It has been reported that some victims of torture have retreated into a fantasy world from which they could not WAKE UP. This world was just like the normal world, except that they weren't being tortured. The only way they could WAKE UP was to find a note in their fantasy world telling them to WAKE UP. Even then it would take months for them to finally discard their fantasy world and PLEASE WAKE UP.

At the time, this was a fairly obscure internet meme that James had discovered somewhere on his cyber travels. We discussed the concepts found in the text of reality and fantasy, but most of all James was attracted by the exhortation to 'WAKE UP.' When he recited the meme, he liked to shout, 'WAKE UP' and I joined him. Together, we often read through the passage and when 'WAKE UP' appeared in the text, we bellowed the words at each other. Luckily, the room was not close to any other occupied classrooms! Eventually, the piece of paper that we had written the text on was enough. We kept it with our other drawings and from time to time James pulled it out to remind himself of it.

Walking through change

I continued to see James as he made his way through school. Adolescence collided with an increase in workload and then exam pressure, and it was tough for him. James remained easy-going and pleasant, but retreated inwards. He became still, quiet and rather isolated. He continued to be only interested in obscure realms of the internet or details of computer technology, and his friends started to run out of things to say to him, as he did with them. He was excited by almost-unwatchable 'glitched' YouTube videos. The visuals of the clips used violently saturated colour, followed no narrative and frequently melted into unintelligible screeching and squawking. It was hard for me too. I couldn't stand the videos, but he would urgently ask if I'd seen them each week. I'd try once again that evening to sit through even one ten-minute video, so we had something to talk about the following session. Eventually, when I arrived at the school to see him, I tended to find him asleep. After a while, I decided to push James first into an upright position and then onto his feet. I suggested that we went for a walk away from the school.

As we walked slowly across the field and out of the school's radius, James started to perk up. He liked to remember our old games and adventures, so we reminisced. I started to point out the nature around us – plants, trees and the occasional animal. From this basis, our conversations, week by week, started to branch out into the subject of shared reality. Carefully, we worked on what James's view of the world was and how it may be different to others. As James patiently described the operating system of a particular computer to me, I realised once again that this was his reality. He described his reality entirely through the language of technology. So, I became more of a translator, curiously checking the details of his 'computer view'. At times, I reflected my interpretations to him completely openly. He agreed or disagreed, made adjustments and reconsidered his position. Each time this happened, I deepened my ability to understand his language and view a little better.

We walked around the local area, at times covering some distance. I tended to steer to footpaths and green areas, but I noticed that James seemed rather more comfortable on pavements. As he revealed the complexity of his world view to me, I began to understand that probably just walking on changing surfaces required quite a bit of care and attention for James. He saw the cracks and stones in the path through the prism of his own 'glitched video'. He tended to rely on his voice as a kind of anchor whilst he was walking. His speech sustained him and enabled him to be in a rhythm that his feet corresponded to. When James took the lead each week, he tended to choose the same route. We walked around a residential area of bungalows with front gardens. Although it can be a problem for autistic people to over-repeat experiences, I became interested in his choice. As weeks turned to months, we were able to notice small changes on our route: seasonal colour, a newly laid driveway. Every now and then, we stopped to check out something that had changed. When James was stationary and in familiar territory, he became able to really *look* at a new fence or a brightly budding tree. He saw that things were moving on and the future was unravelling itself in front of him.

In that period when James was 15 to 16 years old, we spent a lot of time walking, and talking directly or indirectly about autism. The dynamic started to shift. I was a novice in my understanding of the actual reality of living with autism. James taught me, not just about himself, but also about other young people who had similarly unusual interactions with the world. He was kind, patient and always ready to help me understand his unique view. Sometimes he spoke directly from his own human experience, but if he was unable to express himself clearly, he reverted to his preferred language of computers and technology.

REFLECTIONS ON JAMES

When we look at James's story, it's possible to see developmental change over this period of his teenage years, but the change appears patchy. James learned to come out of his technological shell a little. But he didn't deliberately choose to make his interest in technology a protection; it just happened naturally due to a severe difficulty in filtering out sensory information. So, when he started to emerge or at least play with the idea of his shell, he had a lot of catching up to do. This is not about James becoming more 'normal'. He simply needed to discover *any* sense of identity other than that of a 'virtual boy'.

The Virtual Boy

It is too simplistic, no matter how neat it seems, to suggest that James was fascinated with the Virtual Boy because it represented him. Later on in our time together, he himself explained that although he did at times feel like a headache-inducing technological outsider, his interest in the Virtual Boy was multi-layered. Like quite a few autistic teens, James was interested in Japanese culture. He loved the way that, in modern Japan, ideas and design are absolutely synonymous with technology. Something about the cartoon images was also easier for him to take in visually and make sense of. Japanese culture delights too in innocent and joyous childhood. James wanted to explore some of these ideas.

James actually toyed with a few characters as icons in his mind. He was an avid fan of various video-game characters and tried out their voices and images. No one image or character is enough for an entire human being's sense of identity, however. James needed to mix and match, to play and reimagine in order to shape and discover his own sense of self-identity.

When Nintendo made the Virtual Boy, it may well have been a worthy and progressive concept, but it had a fundamental flaw: the extreme graphics rendered it unplayable. So, if we think of James as a games console, he was looking for a way to make himself more 'playable'. He wanted to be able to interact easily with his friends and family and share interesting and meaningful ideas. In order to do this, we needed to tackle his sensory overload first. Otherwise, whatever useful input I or anyone else gave would just be piling more and more undecipherable information into his already overfull inbox.

Bodywork into play

My clue to James needing some bodywork was in his love of being dragged around on the floor wrapped up in a cloth. It was a game, but it didn't go anywhere. James required this activity on a mainly sensory level, so I thought I'd try some other sensory techniques. It's a bit extravagant glamorous to suggest that deep pressure, body alignment and massage are 'magical' in their effects, but in my experience, when delivered well and at the right time, they can be. In fact, it's fair to suggest that the simple routines that are outlined in this story shouldn't, in terms of how the body works, have an especially profound effect. I suspect that the reason why they are so helpful is because they are about 'settling' the body and creating a conducive environment. The body has a good deal of self-healing in its nerve endings, and somehow children are able to find sensory calming and physical relaxation within and for themselves when their bodies are given *permission* to relax, through placing them in the right position and letting the breath and limbs naturally lengthen.

Once the body has a chance to regularly release and relax, the process of play and creativity can begin. This, in teenagers especially, is how identity is formed and reformed – through interactions and play with others.

Steve

James was not sophisticated in his representations of himself. Steve was nothing more than four lines and a circle, but James made sure that he was hard to beat. The interactions between my figures and Steve basically boiled down to one simple message: 'You will never win over me.' For James, this was positive in that he was developing his sense of self-worth; however, there was no flexibility because he *always* wanted to be on top. The way that we played with this was by zooming out. We took a 'meta view' (Sansone, Morf and Panter, 2014) by looking at the unstoppable and unwinnable conflicts between our characters from a very big distance. When looking from the viewpoint of another planet, we can gain perspective and be philosophical about conflict.

Wake up

Whilst teenagers jockey with each other for identity and position, they usually become curious about the bigger questions and correspondingly grow interested in philosophy, science, the arts or politics. James found himself becoming fascinated by the 'Wake up' meme. The text suggests being trapped in a torturous world, but with a prompt to escape by waking up. James was excited by the possibility of waking up and being in a new world. By shouting 'wake up' again and again, he was challenging himself. If he wasn't actually 'breaking through', he was at least playing with the possibility that he could.

I feel that James did want to 'wake up' out of some kind of slumber, but it's hard for any of us to break through a strong personal barrier. Autistic children challenge themselves more than we sometimes imagine, but they tend to do it in a tentative and/or repetitive way. When James was shouting 'wake up' with me, it was a bit like he was knocking on the door of his psyche. He returned to the task again and again, querying and reminding himself. He wasn't really ready for a big breakthrough, but that initiating part of himself was intact and working. In his own parallel way, he was just the same as a teenage girl shouting down the stairs at her parents that she *will* go to the party. The girl in question may not actually make it to the party, but she has to believe that she might.

A shared world, a shared language

It could be argued that the central issue for an autistic person is how to deal with other people. James was slowly but surely making progress as the time passed. He had a devoted and switched-on family and lots of specialist input. But there was an initial issue that remained a feature in his life. James liked to interact, but his chosen interface (repetitive conversation and obscurely technological subjects) was just not connecting with other people, autistic or otherwise. James continued to try. Sometimes he was seen as quirky and was tolerated, but he was also astute; he was aware of the problem and, as he became increasingly isolated, he began to give up.

Once again, we had to go back to the fundamentals of the body. This time, relaxation and desensitisation were not what was needed. James's body polarity had reversed; he was now no longer hyper-stimulated by the world. He was instead becoming dulled to the world, taking an increasingly *hypo*sensitive position, and as a result he was shutting down. So, he needed the upright and steady stimulation of walking.

Walking with autistic teens is one of my favoured approaches. A colleague of mine once came up with the idea of having a string of schools connected along a footpath. Every day the activity would be to walk to the next school. On the way, lessons could be delivered verbally and difficulties shared as the class walked with their helpers, strung out along a beautiful footpath. It's a brilliant idea, because it puts bodily movement at the centre of the curriculum, and there is a simple purpose: to reach the next class by the end of the day. When we walk together, we are *alongside* each other, eye contact is minimised and the voice is not directed straight at your companion's head. Add to this the gentle rhythm of walking and the steadily changing landscape, and you have a desensitising and physically positive activity on which to base the real business of human interaction.

By this stage, I had become very used to James's manner of speaking. He was clear, but nearly always based his statements on something to do with computers or the internet. Because he was used to me too, he had no qualms about jumping straight into his latest obsession (as he himself called them) and not sparing any detail. Whilst this was going on, I was generally wondering, in my mind: Why this topic? And what does this tell me about James? Sometimes I just asked him straight out, but mostly I tried to understand what he meant: what the technology that he was into actually did, and why. As my understanding of his subjects grew, so did my understanding of James. I realised that in some ways my 'therapist's brain' was getting in the way. It meant that I had to translate his language into mine. But just as when we learn a foreign language, there is a point when we jump. We are no longer translating, we just *know* what is being said and we are able to respond directly in the same language. The interface of translation is no longer there; we are simply connected.

Obviously, it might not have ultimately been very helpful to James if I had just become a kind of clone, as equally immersed in this esoteric world as he was. But, in my experience, this doesn't happen. I was still me, I still had my agenda and ways of thinking, but now I could communicate directly with James. The proof that something was working was demonstrated in James's increasing enthusiasm for our walks, even in very unhelpful weather. He didn't need to check that I had seen the latest video or that I agreed with his opinion. He simply enjoyed the fact that someone other than his immediate family understood him. It wasn't long before he started to make forays into my language, my world. He asked me about myself and my interests, and then finally he was able to pay real attention to our shared experience – the environment that we were walking through. He moved smoothly between the worlds, from technology to curiosity about me and then to what we could both see around us. We no longer needed to shout 'WAKE UP' at each other, because we were, finally, awake together.

PRACTICAL POSSIBILITIES FOR 'DEEP PRESSURE'

1. Use a thin gym mat for a child to lie on. He or she needs to feel the floor without it being uncomfortable.

2. When you make physical contact with a child, let your touch be clear and defined, not tentative. Be sure that the child and those around you (e.g. parents) consent to this approach to relaxation.

3. Keep approaches very simple. Line up the body with the arms alongside the torso and carefully press down the lower arms and legs, ensuring that the joints are flat. Ask the child to tell you straight away if he or she feels pain.

4. Those children who have severe difficulty with being touched by another person may prefer you to use a mat or beanbag to apply pressure.

5. Always ensure that the child can breathe easily and enjoys the experience of deep pressure.

7

IN THE MOMENT
Dancing at the Edges

Michael taps the back of his hand without ceasing. His T-shirt hangs low around his neck. Where he tugs and sucks at it, a dark stain spreads out and downwards. His 'words' are the darted flashes of his eyes, escaping from a rigidly held gaze ahead and away from me.

He walks with stiff, straight legs, striding around the darkened hall. His path cuts along the wall. Occasionally, he trails his fingers, keeping time with his stilted steps as he circumnavigates the hall, perhaps counting, perhaps calculating the angle of the lights, the movement of the universe or the exact pacing required to keep as great a distance as possible from me.

I fall in step on the opposite side of the space. We both move clockwise, close to the security of the wall. I match his steps: we ring out a unified tempo on the floorboards. I keep carefully equidistant, on another shore to Michael. The rhythm of our pacing feet is soothing. In the hall, all is certain: we maintain the same space from each other and any change in pace is shared. Inside myself, I am unknowing. What's happening? How long have we been doing this? Does he even know I'm here?

Almost to answer my question, Michael turns on his heel, now pacing anticlockwise. He is careful to do it when we are on opposite sides of the room. He doesn't want to face me yet. I adjust, wheel and turn and we continue. Just at the moment of my uncertainty rising again, he spins again. I turn too. We are clockwise.

This new pattern repeats, either randomly or in a way too clever and subtle for me to follow. After a few rounds, I take a risk.

Michael turns; I don't. We pace inexorably towards each other, round the corner, down the long, straight wall, so that now I see his body shape bearing down on me. I'm careful not to look directly at him. I march on, so does he, and simultaneously we both shift an inch and sweep past each other. We go around the space with our feet drumming and then once more the swish of proximity. He turns again, I remain on my path and now we are both moving in the same, equidistant direction.

There is another sound. It was always there, but I didn't initially hear it over the beat of our feet. It is a muzzled, throaty grunt. It goes in time with our pacing and syncopates the rhythm; not clearly pitched, but it rises and falls. Michael is singing. I follow his lead again and at first just breathe. A little more in my throat, very quiet, but I know he hears me. Is this a tune? A muted conversation with mouths closed. Michael doesn't hang about. He sings louder and turns again, then again. I pitch with him, turn with him. The complexity hits me. I don't know how to do this, I'm in his hands. In this paced-out web.

We turn whilst directly opposite and across the room from each other. Now we are walking together into the centre of the room and leaving the wall behind. I feel exposed away from the solid brick, but Michael is confident: he brushes past me. Just keep up! We find ourselves in opposite corners now, at diagonals; we cross the floor, we spin on the spot in unison. Wait! Where did that come from? We do it again; yes, it's still a pattern. The music is louder now from us both. Vocal rhythm and pitch create a second web that overlaps the first. Not enough for Michael, he breaks into a canter. I do too. Where is he? Yes, I see: he's heading that way, so if I head this way – a triangle, a hexagram, a parallelogram. We sing and dance a cat's cradle in this hall.

We move towards each other once again into the centre of the space. I am now in the flow, ready to weave past and beyond, but Michael stops moving and singing. He stands tapping his hand: clap clap clap. The teacher applauds the pupil. He looks past my shoulder and smiles.

8

PUPPETS TO THE RESCUE

Tony came to my attention with a bang and a crash. He had just started secondary school and was finding the new environment difficult. He was loud and disruptive in the lessons, swearing at teachers and indeed the class in general as he stormed out of classrooms. He was able to access a quieter place in the school, but he wasn't especially calm there either. He bashed things and shouted and became irate with virtually everyone in the place. He couldn't see why he should be in a separate area to the rest of the school, but he also couldn't see why he should be in class. In fact, he didn't want to be in school at all. But instead of not turning up, as some do, Tony was resolutely there every day, in loud disagreement with the whole place.

When I met Tony, he seemed not so much aggressive as reactive. He tended to look for something negative and then be immediately unhappy about it, which made him a stressful person to be with. Certainly, I noticed that I felt edgy around him. Part of my mind was preoccupied with the question: What's about to happen? He was intelligent, quick-witted and most of all hyper-vigilant. He heard and disliked conversations next door, felt that a lot of the teachers and pupils were out to get him, and could be explosively anxious about changes or mistakes on his timetable. He was exhausting and, I suspected, exhausted.

Tony's parents had different racial and cultural backgrounds. Although he was negative about many things, I noticed that he was not automatically negative about his family. They were enterprising people who ran a small family business that Tony was very proud of and involved in. They lived in the countryside and Tony contrasted his life at home with his 'town school'. He felt like a fish out of water in his new secondary placement and was flapping around so much there was a real danger that he would have to leave.

The initial problem that I faced with Tony was what to do. He couldn't cope with just being in a room and talking because the scrutiny of such a situation would have been too intense and focused for him. He would have seen dance as 'weird', and art activities didn't engage him for very long. I saw him pacing from room to room and heard the stories of him storming out of classrooms, which left me wondering if he felt claustrophobic when he was inside. I therefore suggested that we leave the school and go for a walk.

Tony quickly decided to take me up on my offer and marched straight out of the building. At 12 years old, he was big for his age and walked at a quick pace. He had an attractive, angular face with dark eyes and jet-black hair. But I could see anxiety etched across his features as he walked. He held his jaw in a firm line and screwed his eyes up as though everything around him was an assault.

As we left the school behind and walked through quiet suburban streets, he relaxed a little. His shoulders dropped slightly and he talked in a calmer way about his surroundings. I started almost immediately to see a different side to him. He was shy and easily embarrassed, and he had a remarkable amount of knowledge about machinery, local geography and other miscellaneous subjects. He spoke like an adult, but was not grandiose. He was surprisingly open-minded and liked to tell jokes and recount humorous events. I found myself laughing... He was funny!

As we turned a corner there was a line of garages on our side of the road. He glanced at them and declared, 'They're all empty.' When I looked at his face I saw a look of genuine sadness and desolation. The contrast with the joking boy just a second or two earlier was stark.

We headed to a small stream that fanned out over a concrete weir. The water was shallow and he easily managed to walk around and through the stream by stepping on stones. There were bits of rubbish in the weir brought down by the stream. He disliked this and in particular pulled a glass bottle out of the water. I think Tony sensed my concern because he handled it carefully, but he immediately started to talk about smashing the bottle. It was almost as if he thought that this 'rubbish stream' deserved to be punished by having something broken in it. He moved around the weir talking about how he could smash the bottle. I offered a couple of tentative suggestions that involved perhaps *not* smashing the bottle. In the end, I was relieved to see him put the bottle back in the water by sliding it down and along the weir in a precarious but intact manner. When I wrote my notes later, I summed up with one word: 'Volatile'.

How to create a connection

Like the bottle skittling across the concrete weir, so Tony was sliding across the structures of his new school. He was out of control in the classroom and there was a constant possibility that a turn or bump could cause him to shatter. The most important thing in the first instance was to stop his *velocity*: in other words, the speed and recklessness with which he engaged in the school day. Because he was anxious and hyper-vigilant, he tended to charge into situations, sometimes literally. If he could slow down his interactions with the school, there was a greater chance that he would get to the end of the day without incident.

Tony was unable to engage with my standard approaches of calming and relaxing. He was touch-defensive and unwilling to lie on the ground. His mind wouldn't let him focus on his breath or bodily sensations for any time at all. I suspected all along that this approach would be putting the cart before the horse. First, Tony needed to settle himself around people, including me. He was mistrustful of the staff and there was no way things could change until he allowed himself to like, or at least accept, people at the school. I decided to go back to being in a room with him. Claustrophobia is not just about external spaces; it is fundamentally about how we feel internally. I realised that if he could cope with just being together with me in a space, he would, in time, begin to trust me. So, I needed a 'hook' in order to, as the psychotherapist Franco Scabbiolo says, 'fish him in' (Scabbiolo, 2013).

Finding the best hook

I knew that Tony was bright and liked patterns, so I tried playing Mah Jong with him. It's a complicated Chinese game and I thought he might enjoy it. I brought the set of rectangular tiles to the room and in the first instance just opened the box for him to inspect. Before I had managed to explain what the tiles signified, Tony took some out of the box and started to build a structure with them. I immediately forgot the idea of teaching him anything and instead just watched as he constructed small buildings out of the tiles with roofs made of the long plastic chips that are used to score the game.

The following week Tony made a bridge with the plastic chips and tiles. It was precarious and whenever he got close to finishing one he'd destroy it by shaking the table, pretending that it was the movement of running water underneath. I could see that Tony wanted to construct and then play with ideas. Moving in parallel, the school, on my advice, had got some Lego out of someone's attic and left it 'lying around' in Tony's vicinity. Sure enough, he started to make machines with it and the following week he brought them to show me. But when he came in with his Lego constructions, he was very put out. He had seen another child in the special needs classroom playing with a couple of glove puppets. He moaned, 'Why should she have puppets when I don't?' On hearing this, I knew that the following week I needed to bring my own two trusted therapy assistants:

Foxy

Lamby

Foxy and Lamby to the rescue!

The next week, Tony and I went to our usual room with some Lego and he started to construct various objects, speaking a little as he went. Suddenly, we were interrupted by another boy, who was himself quite disruptive. Tony couldn't stand the interruption. He leapt up and went for the other lad. I rushed to put myself between the two of them and managed to get the intruder out of the room. One of Tony's main difficulties was that he couldn't let things go. If he felt that something was wrong or especially if he had a grievance against someone, he pursued it. So, in this situation he was bursting to follow the other boy and have it out with him. I managed to say, 'Hang on a minute, I've got something to show you.'

Not for the first time, Foxy and Lamby leapt out of my bag and to my aid. Tony was instantly interested in them. We tried both of them on, but he settled fairly quickly with Lamby, which left me with Foxy. We played for a while with the idea of who might eat whom, but then he started to pull the Lego models into the game. Tony was able to imagine Foxy and Lamby using the Lego toy machines and driving or riding on them. He was finally hooked. He stayed with me for the rest of the session and left when the bell rang, having forgotten the earlier interruption.

It had taken a month of trying to find something that 'held' Tony. He and I played with Foxy and Lamby and the Lego models for the next year and a half until he finished therapy at the age of 13.

The rules of engagement

Each week, at the end of our session, Tony and I would recap to each other what had happened that week in our glove-puppet game together, in order to try to remember for next week where we would pick up the tale. When we met again, we usually spent a couple of minutes remembering the previous week and then we set to. Sometimes there was a clear ending, in which case we started a new story the following week, but throughout the whole year and a half of work, there was always one clear storyline, which was about the friendship between Foxy and Lamby. At times, their connection was severely tested and there were even 'spin-off' subplots involving other animals who appeared from my bag, but, ultimately, we always returned back to the two heroes of the play.

Playing with children is a serious business. We all like to play, and it's easy for it to become your own story rather than that of the child. Of course, your story does inevitably become enmeshed in the play; indeed, it would be one-sided and sterile if it did not. The best way to describe therapeutic play of this type is that it is 'co-created' (Etherington, 2004) by both of the people involved. I had a couple of parameters for myself. First, I always let Tony start the play. He would have the original idea. One of the difficulties that autistic children face is that they find it hard to develop ideas. They get lots of initial images and themes, but they tend to get lost down dead-ends or in repeated patterns. My role, then, was to make Tony's initial idea interesting and exciting. If, for example, he said that Foxy and Lamby were on a farm, I might say, 'Oh no! What's that combine harvester doing?' If Tony's response was 'Just cutting the wheat,' then I went with that. If, on the other hand, he jumped on that idea, then we perhaps had a runaway combine harvester on our hands. So, my role in the play was to enable Tony to choose new potential vistas that derived from his original ideas. It was only a few months before Tony was able to hold a narrative completely by himself. At this point, I was more a provider of funny voices and special effects. Sometimes Tony became very personally involved in the game and I was able to just observe what was happening and be curious about the themes and emotions that were arising. When I was curious about what his play might mean, I put those questions back into the games to see how he dealt with them. We never directly discussed it, but there were no restrictions to what happened in the story. This meant that sometimes the tales were very dark, grim and explicit, but it also meant that we had no restrictions on finding a way out of difficulty either. Anything could happen in our story: good or bad; weird or ordinary.

The adventure

Once Foxy and Lamby had worked out that they wouldn't eat each other, the next part of the story was about sleep. Lamby especially struggled to stay awake and then, when he did wake up, he was disorientated. As the sessions progressed, this sleeping sickness became more varied, until Lamby was afflicted by a variety of illnesses, such as vomiting, fainting, strokes, stopped heart and a broken leg. Throughout this period, Foxy patiently did his best to look after Lamby, who did occasionally die but then came back to life. Eventually, on his deathbed, Lamby declared that he needed to go back to his family, who were a rare breed of sheep from Norway.

Once Tony got into the idea that we could go anywhere in our play, the storylines became more drawn out and involved. We spent several weeks in the wilds of Norway and encountered many characters, including Lamby's twin brother, who appears again later in the story.

On our return from Scandinavia, it seemed sensible to find somewhere to live. At first, Lamby opted for an apartment; this theme of home ran throughout the play and returned again in different forms. Although Lamby continued to die and be reborn quite frequently, the trip to his homeland seemed to cure his health problems. He became robust and increasingly powerful in his authority. Foxy, on the other hand, was having problems of his own. He was becoming delinquent, drinking and succumbing to his animal nature by eating other animals. Tony suggested that a lot of this behaviour was down to the fact that Foxy was half husky. Although, most of the time, Foxy was Lamby's loyal companion, he did continue to have moments of bad behaviour – after all, eating your friends just isn't on!

A big shift came in the play about three months into our sessions. Tony was making increasingly sophisticated aeroplanes with the Lego outside our sessions. Inside our sessions, Lamby and Foxy started to fly them. Lamby was the pilot whilst Foxy was co-pilot and general 'look-out-for-that-mountain' character. There was a lot of crashing. In fact, after some weeks, Foxy pointed out that they had never managed to get up in the air without crashing back to the ground. Captain Lamby could only take off; he appeared incapable of successfully landing any of the craft that they flew in.

By this time, the sessions were very settled. Tony and I generally spoke about the week at first, but Tony was always keen to get on with the play. He wanted to immerse himself in the story. When he played with the puppets he was completely focused: eyes fixed on what was going on, he barely looked at me, but we constantly interacted with each other through Lamby and Foxy. At times, they were not friends. When Tony had a challenging week, the story could turn dark. Lamby's twin reappeared and became more of a nemesis – an evil twin. Also, Lamby sometimes persecuted Foxy, deriding him for his doggy nature and locking him up. At one point when he had locked Foxy away, Lamby filled Foxy's room with water. Foxy battled to stay afloat, but the water level rose until the tip of his nose was jammed up against the ceiling. Poor Foxy perished. Even when he came back to life, Tony pronounced that he had PTSD (post-traumatic stress disorder).

As always in play, a solution was around the corner. Tony decided one day that Foxy needed to go to see a therapist. At this point, I took Foxy off my hand and Tony immediately put him on his. I took hold of a toy rabbit who looked suitably therapeutic and then we proceeded to have a counselling session. Tony via Foxy was very open about his difficulties in coping with sudden unwanted thoughts and his erratic responses. The rabbit therapist listened carefully and made a few simple suggestions. She also asked to see Lamby, as she pointed out that he may have something to do with the problems that Foxy was experiencing. They arranged to meet again and they did, a few times during the coming months.

Outside the session

It was around this time that I began meeting Tony's parents with other members of his school staff. Over the months that Tony was at the school, he was steadily settling. His staff were getting to understand him, and he was coping better with the routines of the school. At times, there were still difficult days or events, but the general trend was one of gradual improvement. Tony's parents clearly cared a lot for him. They were often bemused by his insistence on being a member of their workforce in their business at home. They described to me that at one moment he'd be out working very responsibly in the yard, and the next he'd be at home shouting and banging about something inconsequential. I suggested to Tony's mum and dad that he was trying to grow up too fast. The child part of him had been side-lined in his own desperate drive to fit in at home and be an adult. He wanted to be an adult because he hoped that it would make him a more steady and reliable person, but instead it created a conflict in him because he wasn't yet able to be the adult that he expected himself to be.

The staff in Tony's school had been working hard with him too. We regularly met and discussed how things were going. They had recognised his sensory needs and were really helping him on that front. They also let him play with Lego when he was stressed, and were starting to create solid and trustworthy relationships. Tony's parents had hit on the idea of him playing drums. He was having lessons at school and the staff were taking him over to the music rooms to practise. The music teacher in turn had noticed his ability and was encouraging him.

When we had our meetings, at first Tony was timid about coming. It was hard for him to see everyone together in one place. It was as if he was being faced by every aspect of himself at once. He was a private person, so I didn't discuss what he and I did in our sessions, but I did say that he found play useful. Tony, becoming emboldened from our meetings with others, clearly told his parents and the staff that he wanted to continue seeing me. It was also an opportunity for me to address Tony directly. I talked to him about how I thought he was doing and what needed to happen next. It was a bit like our therapy sessions with Foxy and the rabbit. But we didn't have them on our hands.

The journey home

In our sessions, we returned to some of our previous themes, but they had transformed in some way. For example, both Lamby and Foxy went to an underwater world. They could breathe and explore and find treasure in this place. Even the catastrophic flying missions improved. Lamby finally managed to land a plane and even Foxy learned to fly. He developed PTSD again from being a

World War ll fighter pilot, but Tony suggested that Foxy could have a small model of his fighter plane to look at when it was night time in order to desensitise him to the trauma. We played this scenario through and, indeed, when Foxy became panicked at night, he played with the toy plane and felt better.

For the last few months, Foxy and Lamby settled on a farm. It was a bustling place with a lot of industry. They encountered various problems, but managed to overcome them by working together and calling on their other friends for help. Eventually, I noticed that Tony was showing brief signs of boredom in our sessions. He lost concentration or stopped to stretch. He also started commenting to me on what was happening in the play as it was going on. He even adopted the voice of Foxy's conscience at times when he was going astray.

The end was coming and it seemed that Tony knew it. In the last few weeks, he said to his staff, 'I don't need therapy any more.' He announced to me one day that he had 'called a meeting' with his parents and he would like me to come. He was in control on the day, being clear about how he was doing in class and what he'd like to manage next. In our final two sessions, we didn't even get Foxy and Lamby out of the bag.

A new horizon

The last time I saw Tony was not in our small room; it was in a large and very full school hall. It was the school talent show and Tony's staff had been working very hard to encourage him to enter. I was there with his mum and dad and his favourite teacher. Tony sat apart from us most of the time, chatting with the other contestants. I was told that he had been playing music with a lot of the other pupils in the school and was getting on really well with them.

We adults were nervous for him, of course, but Tony seemed calm. I noticed only a trace of that determined line to his jaw as he sat behind his drum kit. He played really well, with a natural, fluid talent, helped along by the engagement and encouragement of his peers around him. He was happy to receive a runner's-up prize and, as he sat with his friends at school, he finally looked at home.

REFLECTIONS ON TONY

The art of play

I know a man who is highly skilled and much respected in his chosen profession. At home, his TV is constantly tuned to the children's cartoon channels. Most of the time they play silently in the background, but from time to time he turns them up and watches his favourites carefully. I asked him, 'Why do you watch cartoons and not other TV shows?' He replied, 'Because cartoons are not real. They keep changing in unexpected ways. Roadrunner gets stuck in a safe and then dropped off a cliff, but afterwards he just walks out of the safe. Nobody gets hurt in cartoons.'

This, in a nutshell, illustrates one side of the power of play. The play space is somewhere where anything can happen, regardless of the restrictions of physics and nature. The fact that play is 'not real' means that children and adults can safely explore their greatest fears and aspirations whilst playing. The other side to the power of play is that, although it is pretend, it constantly points at the most important aspects of human reality. We rarely play for very long at mundane things. Something in the way that human beings are wired means that important issues tend to emerge when we play. Play is inherently symbolic and always has meaning. So, the art of playing is to be able to balance the unreal with the significant. When we play with autistic children, we have to find a way to show them that there is meaning in their sometimes repetitive or limited play. If we are too heavy-handed in our interventions, then the feeling of play itself is lost and it becomes a lecture. If, on the other hand, we ourselves become too engrossed in the play with the child, then they may not be able to see how what they are doing is relevant to the other parts of their lives.

Having said this, play is inherently healing. If children who are anxious or depressed are able to play, especially with others, they tend to feel somewhat better afterwards. Like dreaming, play has a way of being helpful to our inner being (Mindell, 1985). When, after we dream, we are able to think about it and reach conclusions, our dream message becomes more concrete in our shared 'real' world. Play is the same. A therapist, parent or worker can help a child make sense of their play, which has an impact on the rest of their lives.

With Tony, I had to approach any reflection on play extremely carefully. He would have become defensive if I had been too keen to talk about what was going on. As a pre-teenager, he needed an adult to just play with him in order to normalise the situation. In the same way as we take care with autistic children to create an environment that is unchallenging to the physical senses, so we also need to make the play environment unchallenging to the child's sense of negative self-judgement.

The fact that Tony himself developed a 'therapy session' with the puppets within his puppet play story indicates that he did not need a lot of help from me in terms of 'interpretation'. He knew that the puppets were doing important things for him personally. We could have endlessly examined the meaning of Foxy being half husky, or having a wild animal nature, or Lamby being unable to land a plane. But that would have impeded the flow of the play and ultimately prevented us from finding solutions through the play itself.

When we are engaged in this kind of intensive play as an adult, we need to find some way of being in the game and at the same time observing it. If I had become too associated with my Foxy character, I would genuinely have PTSD from all the things that happened to me/him. When I'm doing these kinds of sessions, I tend to keep my feet where I can feel them, on the ground. I don't rush to speak and use any spaces in the play to remind myself that I am in a real, physical room. Although engrossed autistic children may not look at you directly much, I make sure that I look at them from time to time. When I see their physical body in the real world, I know that mine is too.

When I am attacked or hurt in the play, I express pretend pain. I show anguish in the puppet and use the removed situation of playing with glove puppets to confront the emotional relationship more. If my puppet has been wronged, he or she will challenge that and want an apology. This may be unthinkable with some children 'face to face', but with puppets, they can do it and more. It's also important to have fun. The more exciting and enticing the play is, the more likely something interesting will happen. But as the adult, we need to be ready for anything. Sometimes disturbing fantasies can come out in the play. At these times, it's best not to add anything to either fix it or, indeed, make it worse. Just being with the child and present in the play at difficult moments can enable them to find their own solutions to the difficulty. This should be the objective. If you are worried that things may get too unpleasant or unruly when playing with children in therapy, it's useful to work with them on a contract.

The therapy contract

There are as many varieties of the 'therapeutic contract' as there are therapies, but essentially a therapy contract is what happens when the therapist and the client formulate the structure and rules that apply to their sessions together. Sometimes a contract may be written. Often it is verbally discussed, perhaps over several sessions. With non-verbal clients, there are very specific difficulties with creating and agreeing a contract, but that does not mean that one can't exist in these circumstances.

Tony was easily able to speak, give his opinions and listen to me. But, as described earlier, he found it hard just to be in a room with me. For him, it was probably an intense sensory and inter-relational experience. Therefore, the first part of our contract was simply about being together. This was during the first few weeks that I described as 'fishing' for Tony's interest and engagement. At this point, Tony was simply getting used to my presence in the room. If I had talked to him about the 'rules and objectives' of therapy at this time, there's a good chance he would have been overwhelmed and simply walked out. The next phase occurred when we started to play with the puppets. Tony decided that this was what he wanted to do every week. We now had a timetable. Again, I could have tried to impose a timetable or structure earlier on, and in fact I did attempt it by introducing the Mah Jong tiles, but it didn't last. In order for a timetable to work, there needs to be a joint acceptance that this is what we're doing and that we want to do it.

Once Tony and I were in full swing with our surrogates, Foxy and Lamby, the third part of our contract came into being: that of a shared language. We had talked to each other a good deal before, but when we played with the glove puppets we created a unique story that only we understood. It was our special language. Once this was established, the rules of therapy were openly discussed through the play. Tony brought a variety of themes to the play that might have been deemed 'inappropriate' by a school teacher. He brought them one by one, testing them out with me. With the puppets, he was saying to me, 'Is *this* OK?' I examined each subject as it appeared and he learned that I would accept it in the story and treat it with the attention it deserved. If one of the toys (usually Lamby) did something extreme or outrageous, we played through all the eventualities: hospital, prison, death, etc. Tony began to recognise that he could bring me any subject and I would evaluate it, work with it and, if necessary, contain it until next week. This is how trust is built. Although Tony was at times angry and thunderous when he came to our session, once he put on the glove, he became contained. Foxy and Lamby contained and played with the pressures and worries that he brought. Having this safe play place to go to also meant that, from time to time, Tony could talk directly to me about problems. We now felt comfortable in each other's presence, we had an acceptance of what it was that we were doing and we had the shared language of play. These three aspects – Presence, Acceptance and a Shared Language – are three essential first steps for creating a therapeutic contract (Torrance, 2003).

Sharing outwards and moving onwards

Once we were really working well with our contract, Tony felt the need to share his progress with his parents and some school staff. I made time each week to talk with his staff, and they were able to introduce some shared ideas into his daily routine. Tony, like many autistic children, was sensitive to the worlds of home and school colliding, but he himself knew that it would be useful. When, later on, he told me that *he* had 'called a meeting', I noted his words. He had put himself right at the centre of his programme so he felt he was in charge of his steady improvement. When a child positively puts themselves in that position, instead of being *done to*, they are *doing*, and progressive change is almost certain.

It was key for Tony to share his progress with his parents. He kept the content of his sessions private, but he shared their usefulness. The staff told me that, one day earlier in our relationship, Tony had stormed out of a lesson, shouting, 'I need to see my therapist!' By the time we came to the end of our year and a half, there was much less storming out of lessons. Tony had brought together the different strands of his support effectively to give him what he needed. Finally, once he was able to make significant relationships with his peers and share musical ambitions with them, he had no need any more for my part of his support. Foxy and Lamby went back into the bag to await the next child who might require their services.

PRACTICAL POSSIBILITIES

1. Play with puppets works particularly well with children who are timid or nervous about owning their feelings. It is also useful with children who tend to become over-excited or dangerous when they engage in physical body play.

2. Puppets do not need to be special looking. A sock on a hand and a bit of imagination is all that is required.

3. Some autistic children prefer to play solely with machines. It is possible to play emotionally and successfully in this way too. Bear in mind that soft toys tend to bring out the soft emotions (sadness, kindness and worry), and hard toys, the hard ones (anger, revenge and triumph).

9

ARTIST IN RESIDENCE

To understand what is going on inside autistic children is half the story. But with some children, especially those who are verbally restricted, it is the hardest half. Getting to know autistic children is not something that we can do by conjecture alone: we have to try things out. Usually we fail, then learn and try again. Children are not indifferent to this investigation; they sense that someone is trying to understand them. Sometimes they do their best to show us something about themselves, or they may resist or leave false trails. But, whenever we closely observe and respond to autistic children, they will in some way give us clues to who they are and what motivates them.

The difficulty with autistic children is that they can appear very contradictory and confused. As a result, the observer can feel contradictory and confused too. What the child is doing (and why) don't appear to make sense. The best way to make sense of someone is by encouraging our own imagination. We need to become creatively curious about what it is like to inhabit this particular child's world. Textbooks on autism can be useful to stimulate our imagination, but the children in question haven't read them. Their perception arises from their own unique experience. We need to enter their personal world in order to understand it. We can encourage these children to join us on this adventure, with the full expectation that we cannot know exactly where we will end up.

The imperative

Leo was presented to me as a boy who couldn't be stopped. He was only nine, but he'd already worked out a formidable way of making sure that his environment was maintained exactly as he wanted it. He was built like a mini rugby player. Stocky and strong, he chose his exact moment to desperately dash and grab or remove objects. Unlike other children, he didn't necessarily avoid people. He often crashed straight through adults and children alike. It was not surprising that the staff at his school felt he needed some attention.

Watching him move, I could see an absolute imperative in his face. He was not 'on the way to' grabbing something. In his mind, he was already there as he moved through space. This is an ability that usually only highly trained athletes can manage, and was also the reason why he seemed so unstoppable. He didn't see the people or objects in his way: he saw only his goal. In fact, if staff were able to hold him back, he still strained forward, head first, eyes trained on the prize. When stopped, he became inconsolable. Something in his sense of the world was broken and he found it very hard to be with himself. He cried and wailed, threw things and hit himself.

It would have made sense to just let him grab an object or rearrange his environment to avoid this distress. At least, perhaps, not to stand in his way might be an option. But when Leo was allowed to fulfil his patterns, it didn't take very long before he was tightening his circle. He restricted himself and the others around him until he didn't even appear to make sense to himself anymore.

Leo had a powerful drive to put things in place. He seemed to have a view of how things should be, and whenever there was a change in the shared world, he moved immediately to put it 'right'. This autistic view started to transfer into his everyday likes and dislikes. He developed a similar imperative about having an extra cookie or *not* having to do schoolwork. Interestingly, his favourite member of staff was quite tough about what was allowed and what was not. It's possible he wanted a boundary. It was as though there was a battle going on inside between two factions. When he was thwarted, he was upset but mainly with himself. He seemed to appreciate having trusted adults to organise him, but at the same time he pushed against them.

Communication is key in these situations, and Leo was getting excellent input from a speech and language therapist. His favourite member of staff was following this up and his parents were engaged and on board. Leo was speaking a fair bit, but it was nearly all repeated snatches of videos and educational games. It was hard to extract much meaning from his speech in general, let alone explanations for his behaviour.

Persistence

I started seeing Leo briefly for just 15 minutes a week as I made a rough assessment of his needs. In the time he was with me, he was cheerful and happy. He liked to play chase games and pull faces. I enjoyed my time with him, but I wasn't too sure it was that helpful to him. Whilst he was with me he seemed to be constantly in a kind of parallel world of videos. After a few weeks, I reckoned that the two of us weren't making much progress and I decided to stop the sessions. For the next couple of weeks, Leo insisted that he still saw me. He wrote our sessions on his timetable and tried to barge into the room when it was 'his' time. At first, I put this down to patterned behaviour; he wanted to continue purely because it was a timetable fixture that needed to be repeated. However, Leo kept insisting. Eventually, I figured, if a child is asking for therapy, shouldn't I respond positively? After a holiday break, I was able to move my sessions around and give him a weekly 40-minute slot.

The sessions

When he came to see me, Leo continued to mimic videos with a faraway look in his eyes, but he engaged readily in several activities. After a while we had a (surprisingly loose) routine. We usually played physical games and wrestled for about ten minutes, then we might dance to music (he especially liked cartoon movie songs and themes); we also sang together and then I encouraged him to relax. We played a going-to-bed game, where we prepared the room for night time. He had a bed high up on a cupboard, whilst I slept on the floor. We had blankets for our respective beds, and from our different places in the room we talked about night times and dreams. His speech and language work was coming on. He was now able to have simple, if rather quirky, conversations.

Drawing

The last 10 or 15 minutes became devoted to drawing. I was already aware that Leo drew a lot. The classroom where he worked was absolutely full of his images, and his teaching assistant provided him with a new wad of scrap paper every day as he fluently depicted repetitive scenes from cartoons. His style of drawing was fluid and minimal. He used a few quickly drawn lines to depict the image in his head. The staff noticed that he became calmer when he drew, but the drawings themselves appeared to be mainly 'evacuation', that is, an opportunity to put down what was in his head. The drawings didn't seem to progress. They were cartoon images, like stills from the original movies.

I encouraged Leo to draw on a large whiteboard. Whilst he drew, I just sat and watched his drawings emerge in front of me. He liked to wipe them off when he was finished, but he would sometimes stand back and admire them for a moment. His drawings were all from cartoon movies and seemed straightforwardly representational, but I started to be curious. Leo clearly had many images in his mind, so why was he interested in these particular ones? A breakthrough came when one day he wrote and then overwrote on the board these words:

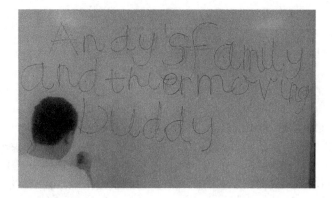

The words probably come from the Pixar film *Toy Story*. In the film, the toys are put into pairs when they are about to move house and they each have a 'moving buddy'. 'Andy' is the name of the child who owns the toys. I later worked out that in the film there's no reference to Andy or his family having a 'moving buddy'. But at the time, I was most struck by the fact that Leo and I had just been dancing all around the room. He said nothing when I suggested that perhaps we were 'moving buddies'. But there was the trace of a sly smile on his face.

When I checked with Leo's favourite teacher, I found that she too had noticed that Leo was occasionally drawing pictures that did not simply represent a scene in a cartoon movie. He was starting to adapt his pictures and 'title pages' to demonstrate something that was going on in his life. He was playing with the images from the movies and using them to show something about his own experience. This was, alongside his speech and language therapy, another avenue of communication. It required translation, but it was a direct line to Leo's inner life.

On another day, Leo drew this on the whiteboard:

As before, this image had a direct link to movement and the body. We had been dancing as usual to cartoon movie songs. At the time, Leo was particularly taken with 'Beyond the Sea', a poignant song from the film *Finding Nemo*. He liked to sing it with me as a kind of duet whilst we circled around the space, spinning together and apart. Our circles of movement connected and disconnected with each other as we danced with the movie's themes of loss, searching and finding friendship.

When the song finished, Leo went to the whiteboard. I settled down on the floor behind him to see what he would draw. Leo started to draw, as usual, a title page from a movie, but he seemed dissatisfied. He stood back and abruptly rubbed it out. He then turned to me and with his distinctive decisiveness, took hold of my hand and placed it palm down on the board. He then carefully drew around it and repeated the process with my other hand. After my two hand prints were on the board, he placed his own hands in the bottom left-hand corner. He carefully drew around his own hands, this time with the back of the hands facing downwards. Next, he virtually knocked me off my feet by trying to grab and lift my foot to the board. I worked out what he was after and pulled up a chair. Whilst I sat on it, he placed and drew around both my bare feet in the centre of the whiteboard. I was unceremoniously removed from the chair and Leo himself sat on it. Try as he might, the angle prevented him from drawing around his own feet, so in the end, he thrust the marker pen into my hand and I drew around his feet at the very bottom of the board.

At this point, with a few clear strokes, he finished his drawing in seconds. Before my astonished eyes, he produced a portrait of the two of us. I occupied the centre of the board, large and imposing but also playful and fun, complete with Mickey Mouse ears and tail. Leo was in a very different position. Small and squashed into a corner, he looked vulnerable, but again, the face tells the story. Then, as well as now, his beautifully drawn face seems to be saying, 'I think I like you, could you like me?'

Leo drew many pictures whilst he was with me. The ones here in this book are some of the very few that he allowed me to 'keep'. He wiped out nearly all his drawings immediately after finishing them. He moved quickly and impulsively. But he liked the feel of the whiteboard – the glide of the pen suited his style, so I didn't encourage him to use paper. The drawings were his speech with me and he wanted his statements to be confidential: only I saw them. Every now and then, as in this case, I persuaded Leo to let me take a picture with my old camera phone. Once he consented, he was quite interested and often made me take a couple of photos at particular angles. He carefully studied the pictures on the phone and then, in a few strokes, wiped the original.

What's underneath?

Leo became more used to drawing with me observing him. He said very little, concentrating on the image as it emerged. Sometimes, he seemed more 'locked' in the cartoon world; he would just produce generic images from his favourite movies. One day I was not especially surprised to see him create a kind of list of Mr Men (another favourite) across the top of the board:

When I looked closer at the picture, I noticed a strange detail: all of the Mr Men and Little Miss characters had a letter inside their mouths. The letters spelt out 'Walt Disney'. This struck me as odd because Mr Men and Walt Disney are different franchises. He would never have seen an image like this one, so for some reason his mind had put these two favourites together. I watched on.

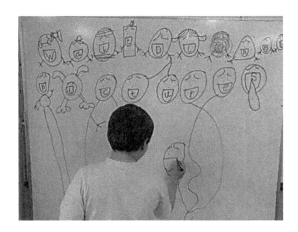

As the picture unfolded, I became more curious about what was happening in front of me. First, you may have noticed that in the first picture of this sequence, Leo has already drawn the face that says 'S' in the second line. He then proceeded to draw the rest of the line of faces and letters after the 'S' face, spelling out the word 'pictures'. This demonstrates a common dyslexic feature of autistic children. He was 'writing' out of order; he started at the back of the line of pictures and then returned to the front. This means that internally he was (probably) seeing the whole image in his mind. It didn't matter to Leo in what order he put things down.

I also noticed that the Mr Men faces were starting to change. They were becoming more of a generic face. It was as though he was becoming bored with his standardised drawing and wanted to get through it. As a result, some of the faces started to shift to something else. I noticed that the 'S' face had a large protruding tongue. The 'P' face had a body, but the legs were trailing away. Leo started to play more with this theme with other faces. They had long trailing streams, heading away down into the depths.

As Leo focused more on the bottom of the board, images started to emerge that you wouldn't find in any children's cartoon. The faces' open mouths had tongues that turned into snakes or hands, holding strange objects. Leo was completely calm, but his worry can be seen in the way that he put a dot within each individual space of the drawing that he created. The result made the characters look almost tattooed. Even down in these depths he put a shipwrecked word, 'presents', sinking down from 'Walt Disney Pictures' above.

Leo continued drawing for some time. He created a whole subconscious landscape at the bottom of the board. It was populated by speckled, disembodied heads, mouths agape and all interconnected by a web of fibrous lines, which in turn connected to the standard heads and letters at the top of the board.

As you can see, I took the first three pictures whilst Leo was drawing. I was close to him and he was aware of what I was doing. But after a while, I felt he needed to be allowed to draw uninterrupted. This was his story and he was revealing it to me alone. I sat back and watched. When he was finished, Leo came to me and I showed him the three pictures that I had taken. He said nothing, but took the camera from my hands and took this last picture, a close-up of a face with another small face held inside its mouth. He then gave the camera back and, with his usual decisiveness, wiped the board clean.

POSTSCRIPT

I continued to work with Leo for a couple of years. He didn't stop being impulsive, but he did become easier to manage and more relaxed. He didn't feel the need to snatch or run off so much. When I think of him now, I see him lying on top of a table, one leg crossed over the other, with his head propped in his hand. He would cast a bemused eye over the scene in front of him and sometimes laugh out loud at the absurdity of something that only he had seen. Leo never used spoken language as his main tool of communication. He was able to ask for things and talk in short sentences, but he preferred just to put things right for himself manually. He could verbally stream whole sections of his favourite movies. Perhaps most importantly, he was much loved at his school and when the time came for him to go on and thrive at a more specialist placement, he was greatly missed as the 'artist in residence'.

REFLECTIONS ON LEO

Me, myself and I

As it says in the introduction, the word 'autism' is a derivative of two words: 'auto', a shortened word for 'self', and 'ism', meaning state or condition. So, autism in its most straightforward sense means 'condition of self'.

Everything in Leo's world at that time was derived from himself. He felt (like young children generally) that he was at the absolute centre of things. If something didn't seem right to him, he fixed it. He did not discriminate between people and other objects or things. Everything was adjusted in the same way, whether it was a child or a table. It's not that he didn't recognise that people were different to objects. He certainly would have noticed that people were far more difficult to organise than other things. But he probably saw everything, from tables to people, on a kind of continuum, which we could call 'peoplethings'.

He probably didn't realise that the 'peoplethings' that got in the way may have had a different view or opinion. He just couldn't see any other view but his own. His controlling behaviour was not really malicious; he was just trying to organise the 'peoplethings', but, it turns out, 'peoplethings' are surprisingly hard to organise. If an autistic child does not realise that they are disrupting others' lives, then their controlling behaviour is actually just an attempt to avoid their own internal chaos.

The chaos that Leo experienced became evident in the way that he drew the creatures on the whiteboard. The top of the whiteboard shows how he maintained a uniformity of idea and view by mentally reproducing particular scenes from cartoons. However, as he descended the board, so he started to reveal his subconscious thoughts and feelings. These thoughts and feelings are more unpredictable and if they are strongly shut out by a powerful thought barrier of movie clips, then things can get complex in the subconscious mind. Left to their own devices, and without any way of being expressed, subconscious thoughts mutate and create new and surprising shapes that demand attention.

We do not necessarily need to 'dig deep' into the subconscious to help somebody. In fact, this experience for an autistic child can be very disorientating. There is, after all, a reason why our subconscious is in the background. We can't function well if unexpected images and ideas are constantly emerging into our everyday life. So, when we look for other ways to help a child, it is a useful starting point to recognise that the conscious mind carries many keys to the subconscious. At the time, I used to wonder, 'Why is Leo drawing these particular images?' Children's movies and TV are full of symbolic ideas, deposited by adults to help children learn and play with the big themes in life. Leo was still in some way sifting through the material and pinpointing what was relevant to him. When he wasn't able to work things out, he tended to draw the image again – to repeat it. It's easy for the autistic mind to get stuck in repetition rather than the process of creative thinking, but true meaning can still find a way through. If we watch autistic children repeating an action, sound or drawing, we notice after a while that each time they repeat there is often a tiny, subtle difference. Change is happening, but it is happening more slowly than in standard child development. This means that often autistic repetitive behaviours are seen as inherently negative, slow or unhelpful. This may be the case, but this method is also the autistic child's own way of learning and processing. Ideally, the child needs to be encouraged to find the most helpful and creative way to do things repetitively. Then the child's development will be owned by him or her and have real meaning.

Hybridising

Leo started the Mr Men drawing by doing something that could be called 'hybridising': that is, putting two different ideas or images of characters on top of each other. This is something that autistic children do a lot. The autistic mind tends to stick in its grooves, so it's hard for an autistic child to think about new things. But they do still want to. One of the ways that the children get new concepts and ideas is by combining existing ones. Like smashing particles in the Large Hadron Collider, the child takes, for example, a Pokémon character and mentally smashes it repeatedly against another favourite character like Super Mario and then finally comes up with a hybrid: Super Pokémon! This is sometimes a very effective way to think of new ideas. Autistic-influenced art forums on the internet are full of various hybridised creatures and objects.

Leo's hybrid was between Disney and Mr Men. Even in the initial images there are lots of interesting features, for example the Mr Men characters speak letters in their open mouths. Speech was a central issue for him because he clearly had many thoughts but found difficulty in saying them. In this ritualised way, his characters/friends were speaking for him.

The mouth, speech and the gateway

The mouth, as discussed in Chapter 2, is an important gateway, and Leo focuses on it in his drawings. The mouth speaks, and Leo was playing with that idea in pictures. But the mouth also reveals things, letters, elongated tongues and even, in the last picture, another being. Is the small head inside another mouth being eaten? Is it being protected or being born? Certainly, with this information it would be easy to create an exciting curriculum for Leo to work on back in the classroom. For example, I encouraged Leo to read anatomy books. He was curious about what was inside himself and others. So, seeing it in pictures was fascinating for him. This was the kind of learning that Leo was receptive to, because the curiosity arose from him.

The moving buddy

The image that Leo drew of the two of us shows a hybridising technique. To allow me into his domain, Leo had to slip me past his mental guards by disguising me as Mickey Mouse. He also borrowed from the physical world and our dancing together by drawing around our hands and feet. It is, in every sense, a piece of collaborative art. It's clear that Leo had learned a lot about faces from watching cartoons. He used that information to plug any gaps that he had from a difficulty in looking at and understanding actual faces. It's also easy to see what's missing: neither character has a body. This is an example of an autistic experience of the human form. Sensory emphasis on the face and hands means that autistic people often have a sense of a gap where various other body parts should be. The feet and hands can simply mark the ends of the body; the interconnectedness of the body from hip to upper leg to lower leg and finally to foot is very hard for autistic children to picture and feel. So, we can see from this image how both external and *internal* communication can be literally disconnected for these children.

When we look down at the self-portrait that Leo made in the lower corner of the picture, we can see, finally, how Leo views himself: the very opposite of the forceful, barging boy who was described earlier; we see a small, uncertain figure, whose hands and face look meek. He could be frightened by the big figure standing next to him, but the faces and eyes tell us that there is a connection. The figure who represents me is friendly and fun. Still, Leo's figure is not sure. But in his face, there is a sign that he would like to connect, if he could just be brave enough.

It takes time to reach these points in therapy. We need to be patient and not jump to conclusions, because it's easy to see how earlier on in our relationship I could have arrived at a very different idea of who Leo was and what motivated him. Luckily, Leo had perseverance. He *insisted* on seeing me, because somehow he knew he needed it. When we, as adults, become set in our own view of a child, we inadvertently restrict their possibility to change. Leo was apparently forceful and self-assured, but we can see in Leo's picture how tentative and sensitive the relationship is. This picture represents the first half of the story and we can see that it was a collaborative effort to get to this point. In order for me to understand Leo, he had to start to understand me. When you 'meet' an autistic child in this way, you really know it. There is not so much a sense of you and I, there is more a sense of 'we'. This powerful experience enables both of us to take the next steps into shared experiences and problem solving.

PRACTICAL POSSIBILITIES

1. Give controlling and anxious children agency over some aspects of their lives, for example, in a part of the garden, or colour schemes in the home. Then be clear about the aspects which you control (your bedroom, food arrangements, timetables, etc.) and those which require joint control (where to go on holiday, when friends come round, etc.). Make a visual map of this like a pie chart with some overlapping areas.

2. Engage your child in 'squiggle drawings' by drawing a line and then asking them to continue your line, and so on, taking turns. At the end stand back and try to identify shapes and images in the drawing.

3. Make laminated speech bubbles which you can place next to drawn characters to help start a conversation and bring them to life.

10

THE WAY OF THE WARRIOR

Therapists who are part of a nationally recognised and accredited organisation are monitored and supervised by experienced and skilled professionals and they are expected to work within a code of conduct. This can be restrictive and time consuming, but it is important. When working with vulnerable children, we need to take very special care, in a general sense, but also from moment to moment within our sessions. Therapists can be seen as knowledgeable and experienced, and as a result it may be hard for our clients to imagine that we get things wrong or fail, but of course we do. In fact, it's pretty much impossible not to make mistakes when working in complex and emotional situations. As a result, I often find myself saying to the children I work with, 'Tell me if I'm wrong…' Interestingly, quite often autistic children may not tell me I've got it wrong, even when I patently have. There are various reasons for this, but one is quite simply that they *want* me to be right. They want to pin certainty onto me because that way they too can begin to feel more certain about things.

So, it needs to be recognised that therapists are the same as everyone else: zigzagging through trial and error in the general direction of a better situation. When we get things wrong, we also learn acceptance, humility and new possibility. When we fail or make mistakes, possibilities appear in ways that we could never have previously imagined.

First contacts

I first met Jason when I was invited to a school. The staff at the primary school were struggling with a boy and felt that they needed some training in behaviour and autism. In these situations, I always ask to meet the child and also encourage the school to invite the parents of the child along to the meeting. This way, I find that I have at least some idea of what the boy or girl is like and, also, when the parents are engaged, there is a greater possibility of agreement about any planned approach that the child may require.

The school was large and modern. It had a nice open feel; the cohorts of children in their classrooms were visible and audible from the central corridor. I knew that although this works well as a working social environment for many, it can be a huge sensory distraction for an autistic child. The staff seemed friendly and engaged with Jason. They took me to his classroom and I immediately bumped into him in a small anteroom. He was standing amongst the coats that were hanging up in a row. It was clearly a difficult moment. Jason had come out of the classroom and was caught in a kind of limbo; he couldn't cope with what was happening next door, but at the same time was not happy with where he had placed himself.

Luckily, Jason was interested in having a visitor and it was suggested that he show me around the school. He suddenly became very switched on and charming, with a considered and mature way of speaking for an eight-year-old. He had straight blond hair, and I thought he looked rather 'cool', mainly because he was wearing a pair of wrap-around shades. The glasses, he explained, were necessary due to his light sensitivity. He moved in a faintly jerky way. As he swept me through the school, I had the impression of someone who was very much in charge: someone who knew what was going on and was endearing, without being pompous. He asked me interested questions and gave thoughtful answers to mine. He told me that he was going to show me 'his room', and with great ceremony he ushered me into a walk-in store cupboard.

The cupboard was probably about three metres by four metres. It was full of school equipment, mainly art materials that were stacked high on shelves all around. Jason closed the door and immediately settled himself on a small chair in the available floor space. I perched next to him. With the door closed, the hustle and bustle of the school was diminished. I realised that, for the first time since I entered the school, it was quiet. Later on, the staff assured me that they had tried to encourage Jason into more suitable spaces, and I believed them. Jason had clearly chosen this space himself. He was comfortable here and, once in his cave, he chatted away to me about himself and his life and also the problems that he had.

At the meeting after school, I met Jason's mum. She didn't say a great deal; there were a lot of staff there and a pretty long list of Jason's misdemeanours. He was violent and also tried, with some success, to run away from school. Jason's mum understandably looked uncomfortable. It's tough being the 'representative' of someone you love who at the same time has been causing a lot of trouble. When I asked her for her opinion, she was thoughtful and deeply knowledgeable about her boy. She was clearly working hard with him at home to try to keep him in school.

I did not see Jason again for about a year. The next time I bumped into him, he was having a transition day to a specialist school where I was working. He was there with his mum, having lunch and getting to know the other autistic children. He remembered me and I him. I sat with them for a while. Jason was overtly friendly with the other children, chatty and trying hard to engage. Some of the others responded, but one boy was glum and negative. Eventually he commented that something Jason had said was 'rubbish'.

I noticed that Jason's mum, who had been observing everything carefully, moved very slightly towards Jason. She murmured to him something about finishing lunch. Jason, at the same time, was changing colour. At first his ears and then his cheeks were becoming pinker. His voice raised slightly as he emphatically told the other boy that what he had said was *not* rubbish. With a skill that's born of experience, Jason's mum deftly cleared up the lunch things and placed herself between the two boys. She focused completely on her son and with a soft voice managed to get him out of his chair and out of the building. Their visit was clearly over for the day.

Setting up the session

When Jason came to his new school in the autumn, it was suggested that I see him for therapy. Jason was willing, having known me a little at his previous school. We sat together in a small room and he chatted away, telling me his story. Jason came from a large and stable family. For him, home was his refuge; he was very fond of both his mum and dad, but he was especially connected to Mum. He occasionally quoted her as he explained to me why he did the things that he did.

The staff in the new school explained to me that Jason was 'tricky'. He was mostly easy-going and engaged, but some days he would become very stuck. At these times he refused to do anything and pedantically argued with the staff about any suggestions that they made. If other children got involved, Jason could quickly escalate; if the situation wasn't dealt with immediately, fights could ensue – and Jason was strong and determined. Unlike some others, he often held a grudge and insisted that he was in the right. On the occasions when Jason really got out of control, he sometimes broke down and was extremely unhappy. He would say he was useless and tearfully talk about ending his life.

After a few sessions with Jason, I started to wonder if martial arts might be useful for him. He was someone who had real difficulty controlling his emotions and his anger, and he was also very keen to find a better way to live. He wanted to be his usual pleasant self and didn't want to be a tyrant. When his tyrannical self emerged, he felt disconnected and then later hated himself. It seemed to me that he needed to integrate these different parts of himself in order to feel more whole. At the same time, martial arts might help him with self-control, enabling him to keep himself in check on a day-to-day basis whilst he explored who he was in more depth through therapy.

Jason was keen on doing martial arts straight away. I tried a couple of simple exercises with him and he engaged enthusiastically, perhaps too enthusiastically, as he almost immediately decided that he was going to be really good at martial arts, probably better than me in fact!

The first thing to do was to phone Mum. When I suggested to her that I'd like to try martial arts with Jason there was silence at the other end of the phone. Mum had spent many years working very hard trying to keep Jason's violent outbursts to a minimum, and certainly needed convincing that training her son to be a ninja was a good idea. She had a younger child and was no doubt concerned about his safety. We discussed the idea and I explained that by doing martial arts, Jason would have a chance to explore the uncontrolled part of himself, which might, in turn, lead towards him becoming less violent. I said I'd be very careful and there would be rules, the most important of which would be that if Jason used a martial arts technique 'in anger' outside the session, we would stop the training within our session.

Mum, to her credit, agreed and we both made sure that we stayed in close contact to see how things progressed.

The way of the warrior

Jason was an imaginative and verbally active child, so right from the start, along with the martial arts training, we had discussions and storytelling about the world of martial arts. I deliberately introduced him to Chinese Kung Fu, which is packed full of stories and images. When we practised the base postures we also discussed the meanings of 'Horse Riding Stance', 'The Cat' and 'Tiger Stance' (Kiew Kit, 1996). I casually introduced him to the Chinese names of postures so we had our own special way of referring to them. Jason found static stances very difficult. These stances deliberately place the body under pressure, especially the large muscles of the legs. They are as tough mentally as they are physically, and to progress you have to bear it. Jason had to learn tolerance. In order to move on, I gently insisted that he first try these postures, so from the very beginning the idea of discipline was embedded into our sessions.

Next, Jason and I worked together on forms. In Chinese Kung Fu, there are almost countless sequences of movement, strung together into martial dances, which are commonly known as forms. We concentrated on animal forms: the Tiger, Dragon, Eagle, Mantis and so on. This ignited Jason's imagination and kept his concentration up whilst he painstakingly learned the sequences of various forms.

Whilst he was engaging in this traditional Kung Fu, Jason was also itching to fight. We again tended to keep this within the confines of the form. For example, when I showed him the next move in the form, I also showed him its application, that is (in terms of combat), what the move might be used for. We practised these simple strike-and-defend combinations several times for each movement. But Jason wanted more; I suspected that in this safe and calm environment he wanted to feel the sensation of open physical conflict. In order to do this, I first taught him how to calm himself by learning a simple breathing technique.

In the technique he stood with his feet at hip-width apart. He then inhaled whilst bringing his arms up above his head in a flowing circular motion. As Jason then exhaled, he let his hands, palms facing to the ground, slowly release down in front of his body. By the time his outbreath was finished, his hands were together, facing down at his waist. We did this together three times as a way of re-centring ourselves and encouraging the parasympathetic nervous system (Stahl and Goldstein, 2010, p.28).

When 'sparring', we had a 'stop' signal (simply saying 'stop') that either of us could use at any time. In addition, we bowed formally to each other at both the beginning and the end of our sparring. All of these techniques helped Jason differentiate the 'fighting space' from the rest of our session. When we did spar, we did not wear protective gear; instead we opted to keep blows very light. We just touched each other lightly on the torso as a way of showing we could get through the other's defence.

Jason relished sparring with me. He was able to put his pent-up feelings directly into aggressive action, but in a safe and constructive way. Like so many autistic children, he hated losing, so I ensured that he was able to get through to me physically and have the 'success' of contacting my torso. It was not that difficult, as Jason moved with a lot of speed and determination. He had a natural disposition to learn in this physically interactive way.

Fairly quickly, a problem arose. Jason seemed convinced that he was nearly on a par with me. Bearing in mind that I was a fully grown man and he a ten-year-old child, this seemed faintly ludicrous. Ordinarily, a teacher can remedy this delusion by just increasing his or her own technique – moving a little faster, using different combinations and so on. I did this, but Jason found it hard to recognise these changes. He just became more excited and even more sure of his ability. It seemed that the only way to get through to him would have been to get heavy-handed, which obviously I didn't want to do. The answer, in the end, was to just keep going.

When Jason became exhausted by the activity, he began to regard me with more respect. He was not fully ready to accept his lesser skill, but he did at least recognise my tenacity.

From time to time when sparring, we would clash abruptly. At these times Jason sometimes banged his arm or shoulder. When this happened, I paid him close attention, making sure he was all right. I was kindly; I didn't want to be harsh, as martial arts teachers can sometimes be. I knew that Jason was tough enough on himself and he didn't need me to add to it. Jason recognised pain. He was brave and usually quickly recovered, but the experience of being hurt did not necessarily change his behaviour. He continued to spar fast and recklessly. I knew from experience that a neuro-typical child would learn these lessons very quickly, often instantaneously. For Jason, the learning needed more time.

The sword that cuts through illusion

Jason was doing well enough in his weekly martial arts sessions, but something was missing. He engaged imaginatively with the forms, but found sequencing movements very hard. He struggled with his executive function (the ability to string events together from beginning to end) (Dodd, 2005) and he needed frequent breaks. He remained conceptually enthusiastic, but his physical learning process tended to be lost from week to week and he had to start again.

I knew from previous experience that it can be useful to introduce an object when doing dance movement therapy with autistic children. Often, the child is able to centre themselves in and around something that they can hold, because they feel more integrated and able to respond to an object. With this in mind, one day I brought in two 5-foot-long sticks. They were constructed of plastic pipe and were surrounded by a foam layer, which made them solid but relatively soft. They are specially made for martial artists to practise staff and sword work without damaging each other, and I thought that Jason might find them useful.

As soon as Jason took hold of one of the sticks he was in his element. I let him just experiment with it outside. He leapt around, arcing and spinning the stick in every different direction. Wherever the stick went, his body naturally followed. I saw him move in spontaneous and fluid ways that I had not seen before. As always, Jason was keen to learn, so in much the same way as before, we divided the time up into learning postures and then practising forms with a stick, before sparring. There was an increased risk with the sticks, so Jason and I had to stop frequently and remind ourselves to slow down and take care. Holding the stick excited and energised Jason, so it was hard for him to contain himself when sparring. He loved the clash of the two sticks, the thrust and parry. I had to be on my toes. I could just about protect myself, but I wanted to be sure that Jason didn't get hurt. I used the forms to help him. As Jason learned standardised ways of using a stick, so he became less erratic and our sparring became more regulated.

From then on, the sticks were at the centre of our sessions. We still practised hand forms, but we incorporated the sticks wherever we could – in posture work, sparring and so on. Whenever Jason had a stick in his hand, he moved better and had a stronger sense of purpose. This spilled over into our discussions too. Jason talked about weapons in general and related them to computer games. The martial arts were creating a place for him to deposit and understand these violent ideas that he found within himself.

Incidents

Throughout the two years or so when Jason and I practised martial arts, the staff at his new school were also working hard with him. He once described this school to me as 'like a comfortable queen-sized bed'. They nurtured him, focusing on his many talents and generally kindly nature. He also built up a strong relationship with a speech and language therapist, and she and I consulted regularly on his progress. As a result of all this, he was settled and his outbursts had reduced in number and intensity, but they still happened. Whenever he had a stand-off with staff, they reported it to me and I was glad to hear that he didn't use any techniques that he had learned with me. Nevertheless, he and I maintained a dialogue about his behaviour and how his work with me was designed to improve it.

Unfortunately, one day things got out of hand. There was a fair amount of conflict going on between various pupils in the school. Jason was involved and he became very aggressive, which culminated in him kicking and bruising one of the members of staff. When I was told the story, I was mortified to hear that the kick that did the damage to a particularly loved and experienced member of staff was not spontaneous or 'lashed out'. It was a martial-arts style 'roundhouse kick' of the type that I had been teaching Jason in his forms.

The member of staff in question was very good about it. She, like most people who work with autistic children, had experienced this kind of thing before and was solely focused on what was best for Jason. Nevertheless, I knew that Jason and I had just received a very clear message that something in therapy was not working correctly, and I needed to take a long, hard look at what we were doing. He and I sat quietly together in our room. Jason was very upset and remorseful when we discussed it. He cried when he thought about the member of staff and he said that he'd let me down. Of course, I felt that I had let Jason down. Somehow, I hadn't spotted this coming, or perhaps I hadn't focused enough on the right areas? We both agreed that this meant we had to stop doing martial arts. Jason accepted his sanction unreservedly.

When, with a heavy heart, I went to phone Mum, I was surprised by her reaction. Over the two years that Jason and I had been working together, she and I had communicated many times and had got to know each other. She also had the perspective of what Jason said to her when he came home from school in the afternoons. She agreed that the incident was a setback, but encouraged me to recognise how important the martial arts training had been for Jason. I had, by now, a very strong relationship with him, forged in the fire of Kung Fu; we had worked and sweated many hours together. Jason's mum knew how significant this was to him and told me so.

In the end, we decided to have a hiatus, a few weeks until the end of term, after which Jason and I would re-evaluate to see if he was safe enough to resume his training. In the meantime, we would focus on other activities in our sessions.

Another pathway to the same destination

Of course, Jason and I had not spent all of our time up to this incident doing martial arts. Sometimes he was ill or tired, and we engaged in other activities instead. One of these was the ancient

Chinese game of Mah Jong. It fitted many of the themes found in martial arts: you had to create sequences with the tiles; it was full of oriental imagery; and it was deeply competitive. Autistic children find the game helpful in a variety of ways. It requires fine motor skills in manipulating the tiles, and it has aspects of sorting, number and serialisation that are so central to development (Solomon, 2012). It also uses symbolism and requires good social skills and turn-taking. Most of all, there are many different ways to win. This means that you can, in essence, win and lose at the same time, which is a centrally helpful learning experience for some autistic children.

Jason loved to talk whilst playing the game together, so we turned our attention for the next few weeks to Mah Jong. We had a book in which we kept scores, and week by week we checked back to see how we were doing. As Jason became more familiar with the game, I was able to introduce him to its more esoteric aspects. He became skilled and interested in the history and the connections with an ancient culture. We learned the names of some of the tiles in Chinese and he collected his favourites: Green and Red Dragons, plus the ever-mysterious White Dragon (a completely blank tile).

After the holiday, Jason was not especially keen to restart his martial arts training. He was comfortable playing Mah Jong and talking about life. He was also probably worried that he might have a relapse of his behaviour. We carried on for a while longer, but I suggested after some more weeks that we try martial arts again. We approached it gently, focusing more on the softer Tai Chi styles. I introduced him to 'Chi Sau' or 'Sticky Hands' (Edwards, 2005), which is a flowing form of sparring where you stay contacted with your partner and work with their movement to unbalance them. In time, I also introduced aspects of Aikido, a Japanese style of martial art that focuses on movement, gravity and energy (Ueshiba 1991). We worked with contact much more, rolling from movement to movement softly with flowing energy.

Into the future

Jason himself chose to vary his sessions between martial arts, Mah Jong and more standard counselling-style approaches. Sometimes we touched on all of these activities in one hour, but he was more in control. His focus somehow shifted from 'See what I can do?' to 'What can we do together?' Naturally, he continued to have stand-offs and problems with other children and staff, but he became more controlled and they were rare occurrences. He never used a martial arts technique outside our session again.

As he reached the end of his time at primary school, Jason became more of a philosopher; he was especially engaged by humanity and relationships. His deeply caring nature became more available for people outside of his tight circle to see. After some years of avoiding schoolwork, he started to demonstrate a real skill in mathematics. Throughout our ups and downs, both Jason and his mum stayed loyal to me. They showed faith in my ideas when others would have condemned them as pointless or ill-judged. It can sometimes be lonely as a therapist, and without the support and connection of our clients and their families, we can feel isolated. When the problems and mistakes emerged on our journey, Jason and his family were there to offer me reassurance and give me licence to stop, reassess and try again.

REFLECTIONS ON JASON

Conflict

All therapists work with conflict, but only some work in the dynamic, physical way that it is described here. The risks of taking this approach are clear, but the advantage is that we go straight to the heart of the matter. When working in this way, we have to balance up the risk against the advantage. We also have to keep the agenda of reducing or transforming conflict on the table. Autistic children generally need things to be clear, and so we need to tell and show them that we are doing *this* activity to help with *that* problem.

Jason was clear about the agenda from day one. He got into conflict with others mainly due to an inflexible attitude and an overly defensive reaction to what others did and said. But, in fact, the central conflict was not really with other people. We can see from the story that Jason was conflicted within himself. On the one hand he was charming, helpful and intelligent, and on the other, abusive, unkind and rigid. This stark dissonance within was really disturbing him. He tried to avoid it as much as he could by focusing on 'nice' Jason, but this meant that when 'not nice' Jason emerged it was in an uncontrolled and pent-up form. When he engaged in martial arts, he had an opportunity to do aggressive things whilst not feeling wholly aggressive. In a similar way to Sandy in Chapter 5, we can see that I was taking Jason to this aroused, fighting place and then encouraging him, whilst there, to develop a little bit of self-awareness. The hope was that this desensitising experience might translate out of our sessions and into the conflicted environments of his everyday life. This worked to some extent, but he also translated the physical movements out of the session and kicked a member of staff. A therapist will work towards acceptance of a client's actions and an equanimous attitude to what they do and say, but this needs to be tempered with basic moral standards and also, in this case, the fact that Jason was a child. I didn't need to pronounce judgement on him in this instance, because he knew he was in the wrong and with his self-negative attitude he almost demanded a 'punishment'. I had to be especially careful at this point because I also felt to blame for teaching Jason in the first place.

In the end, Jason and I faced it together. It was probably a powerful experience for him to hear an apology from a respected adult, but this, as children, is how we learn to apologise ourselves. With support from Mum and the staff around us, we all worked together to develop a safer method of helping Jason with his conflicts.

Teaching or therapy?

Practically speaking, once Jason and I had decided what we wanted to do, I divided the weekly session between the straightforward teaching of martial arts and the reflective skills more usually connected with therapy. We probably did about 30 to 40 minutes of skills-based physical work and then 15 to 20 minutes of mainly verbal reflection before and/or after. The scheduling was organised therefore, but how we approached teaching and therapy was more fluid. Whilst I was teaching, I was constantly curious about how Jason interpreted what I showed him. So, as I taught him, Jason was teaching me about autism, about being a child and, most of all, about himself. Particularly when we sparred, there was a constant physical and psychological connection between us that is truly unusual for autistic children. At one point, I explained to him that the best way to see my strikes coming was not to focus on my hands but to look into my eyes. Any boxer knows that the eyes betray a coming movement, more than any other part of the body. Jason took this on board and from then on willingly locked his eyes onto mine for minutes at a time. Undoubtedly, these experiences served to connect us in powerful ways.

Ultimately, therapy should always be a learning experience. Autistic children tend to learn spontaneously at unexpected moments, so a therapist needs, in these circumstances, to be able to adopt a teacher's position where it's needed. This flexibility and the ability to not be stuck in one's own paradigms is the way to be truly available to a child. I avoided the authoritarian styles of a martial arts teacher in order to protect my persona as a therapist. Teachers of autistic children tend to get the best results when they use gentle and persevering interventions.

History and identity

Autism has been around for as long as there have been human beings, but this modern and European-based view of it that we call 'autism' is less than a century old. When handing out diagnoses to so many children in countries around the world, diagnosticians need to be mindful about where they 'place' that particular child and family with this relatively new concept and label. In some ways, it's fresh and exciting to be autistic. I have had many conversations with people who are enjoying inventing and adapting their own 'brand' of autism that is particular to themselves. But others feel more lost. As autistic people, they don't have much sense of identifiable history beyond vague allusions to Einstein and Sir Isaac Newton. Martial arts, on the other hand, does have a long, powerful and tangible history. When we practise a Kung Fu form we immediately plug into a set of movements that have been practised by countless people through the ages. The forms are created from an often unknown master and then passed down, carefully preserving the essence of the form, from teacher to student, for sometimes thousands of years. An ancient game like Mah Jong also has this quality; the tiles have been handled by generations of people as they gradually adapted the games around countless tables in the Far East.

When Jason started his first tentative movements of the Eagle form, or he collected together three tiles into a 'pung' of Red Dragons, he was touching that history. As he developed the hand shapes and postures of the Eagle form, he started to feel the same thing that many others had felt before him: the power, speed and agility in the form and in the *people* of the form. This is a remarkable experience for anyone, but for an autistic child, more than anything else, I feel it says: *You are not alone.*

PRACTICAL POSSIBILITIES

1. Practise honesty between home and school. If things aren't going well, say so. But don't cast blame. Both school staff and parents can say what they find hard to deal with and openly ask each other for advice. This creates more direct communication, which is useful in times of crisis.

2. If the standard methods of communication between home and school are becoming tired, try new ones. Send in a picture of a home event or object, perhaps a type of food that was made, and the teacher can ask the child about it.

3. Set up an autistic role model display on the wall. Include photos of well-known and famous people, but also add ex-students of the school, or teachers or family members who identify as autistic.

11

YOGA
Going Inside to Get Outside

One day I received a call from a social worker. She was looking for someone to work with a 16-year-old girl who had 'challenging behaviour'. The girl was no longer at school and for some months she had been at home with her mother and father. The social worker explained to me that although she was affectionate with both her parents, it was only her father who could control her when her behaviour got out of hand. Unfortunately, the girl's father had a heart condition and the strain of looking after her all the time was seriously affecting his health. Respite for the family was desperately needed, and for this reason the social worker was looking for someone with experience of challenging behaviour who was willing to spend time with the girl outside of the home.

At that time, in the early 90s, I was not yet a trained therapist, but I had built up a small reputation for myself as someone who could at least cope with challenging behaviour. The social worker was keen; she had already found a residential home for adults with learning disabilities that was willing to accommodate us during the daytime respite hours. I agreed to meet with the family and the social worker.

We met in the residential setting. Like many residential homes of that era, it was not purpose built. It was simply a large house on many floors that had been previously owned by the church. When I stepped through the doorway there was a distinctive smell of wood polish and disinfectant. The staff were welcoming and I think rather curious about me and their new potential day resident.

I was ushered into a small office and after a short wait there was a commotion outside the door. I could hear a man's voice and through a frosted-glass panel see a figure steering and holding another figure as they careered around the room outside. In the next instant, they were through the door. Mary (the girl) and her father simultaneously burst into the cramped room, with the social worker hovering behind. Mary's dad was holding her back but she easily slipped forward and immediately sat straight on my lap. She smiled a broad smile, her head swinging rhythmically from side to side. Mary's dad, looking relieved, said, 'Oh well, she likes you then.' And it seemed that the deal was done.

Mary had a diagnosis of autism and a severe learning disability. She was a thickset girl with cobalt-blue eyes and strawberry-blonde hair cut into a simple bob. That day, like most others, she was wearing a red sweatshirt and black tracksuit bottoms. She smiled a lot of the time and liked to look deeply into people's faces. She was very impulsive in her actions and moved in a slightly rigid and stop-start manner, rather like a clockwork toy. Her one area of flowing movement was in her head and hips. When she was happy, she swung her head and sometimes her hips from right to left. Her legs stayed stock-still at these times as her upper body swung from side to side. Mary's father was very likeable. Like so many parents that I have met, he had completely devoted his life to his quirky daughter. He too had a broad face and ginger hair, but his face frequently flushed a dark red from both the stress and the frequent exertion that he had to make to keep up with his lively daughter.

The challenge

I arrived at the residential home every morning, and once most of the residents had gone off to their various day settings, the bell rang and Mary would rush in with her dad puffing, slightly behind her. Dad and I spent a bit of time catching up on the night before and then he left me for the day in the large house with Mary.

All parents of children with various disabilities know the feeling of time hanging heavy on their hands. As part of the deal, the residential home fed us and cleaned up after us, so there was rather a yawning gap to fill each day. Mary was always active and curious. She liked to explore the house, going from room to room as though she was looking for something but not finding it. She didn't say a word the whole time that I knew her, although when she was angry she growled, and she chuckled when happy. Mary had been taught a sign language called Makaton (Pollard, 2012), which had a variety of simple hand signs and gestures for everyday objects and activities. She only ever used a thumbs-up sign or brought her hand to her mouth and then back down, which technically means 'please', but she used it more generally for 'I want'. As a result, I had very little to go on as I followed Mary around on her explorations. She seemed to be interested when I spoke but gave no sign of any response. She just carried on her way.

It was inevitable that some kind of problem would arise, and sure enough it did when, one morning, we reached a walk-in store cupboard. A cleaner had left it open and Mary went straight in, running her hands along the items on the shelves. I was aware that there were quite a few things in the cupboard that could be dangerous. Mary actually was most interested in a safe item – toilet rolls. She ripped open a packet and, with a look of glee on her face, started to unroll all the paper, strewing toilet paper around the space. With several industrial-sized packages of toilet rolls in the cupboard, I could see where this was going. She was happy, but I knew that something had to be done.

Whilst standing next to Mary, I quietly said that it was time to leave. No response. Mary reached for another toilet roll and started to unravel it. I placed myself between her and any more toilet rolls. Mary cheerfully liberated the second roll and tried to push past me to get more. I said, 'No more toilet rolls.'

I saw a sudden change on Mary's face. Her response was rapid, but oddly matter of fact. It didn't seem at all personal as she snatched up a heavy metal stool with wheels on it and brought it down with all her strength on my head.

Stupidly, I had got myself into a position where I had no chance of moving out of the way. I had the presence of mind to protect my head with my arm, and that is what took the blow. The stool, being metal, was undamaged, but I wasn't so sure about my arm. It really hurt. And with a sinking feeling, I thought, 'I've got another six hours of this to go today.'

Mary seemed to think that she had made her point and she calmly walked out of the cupboard. I took the opportunity to quickly shut the door and joined her. She looked at me quizzically and I became aware of a strong throbbing in my arm. I crossed the floor to a sink and gingerly rolled up my sleeve. I placed my aching arm under the cold tap and just stood, feeling some relief. I was also aware that adrenaline was pumping around my own body. I didn't feel especially angry, but I knew I had to be careful in what I did next; I had been involved in situations before that had spiralled out of control because everyone there – the child and the staff – was in a heightened state.

Mary was curious about what I was doing and came over to see. She looked with some surprise at my arm, which was red and swollen. I said, 'You really hurt me Mary. Look what happened to my arm when you hit it with the stool.' Although she didn't speak or make any sound, it seemed that she understood something. As it turned out, the next six hours were not so bad; Mary did not continue to search around the house creating mischief. She became more stationary and we sat together playing table-top games and making Angel Delight. Every now and then she got me to show her my arm again. She knew not to touch it, but she sat staring intently, looking at the developing bruise, her nose just centimetres from my skin.

Making a routine

Although Mary and I had a roof over our heads and food in our bellies, it quickly became clear to me that we needed activities that made the day interesting for both of us. I consulted with Mary's father, but it turned out that her unpredictable behaviours had made life at home pretty limited too. Often, in desperation, Mary's father put her in the car and just drove around for hours as Mary stared out of the window. Over the next few days I tried a few ideas. They were all based in the home because Mary's behaviours were too unpredictable in public places. We tried various art activities, which went all right, but generally required a lot of setting up for just a couple of minutes of activity before Mary became distracted. We had more success with games, but they were basic: rolling a ball, blowing on each other's faces and peek-a-boo-type activities worked best. Mary also liked listening to music and she could be engaged in cookery as long as the results were fairly quick in arriving.

The activities still had a production line feel to them. Mary would arrive in the morning and plough through all the activities that I could think of in about half an hour. I had learned how to keep difficult items out of reach and how to head Mary off before she became challenging, so generally things were fairly peaceful. But there was no structure and the days felt aimless. I decided to consolidate the activities into what worked best and create a clear timetable around them.

I had already tried a bit of simple yoga with Mary and she had seemed quite interested. I also noticed that Mary was generally in a heightened state when she arrived in the morning. She rushed in from the car and remained agitated whilst her father handed over to me. I found that if things became difficult, the problem would generally occur in the first hour of the day.

I decided to start the schedule from the moment Mary arrived. I set just five minutes for the handover. Then Mary and I went to make a drink, and she went to the toilet. After that first 20 minutes, we went to the very top of the house where it was quiet, and we had a yoga session.

Yoga

It's now commonplace for yoga to be part of the curriculum for children with special educational needs, but back then it was certainly more unusual. There were no books or advice; however, luckily, I had previous experience of teaching yoga with disabled adults. Those were large classes in halls with usually two or three teachers. This was going to be very different because I could gear it completely to Mary's needs.

I made an initial decision to do all the yoga seated on the floor. This was partly practical, as Mary was not terribly well co-ordinated. Also, once she was on the floor, she was less likely to get up and wander around. Being on the ground also meant that there was a strong emphasis on de-escalation. The yoga session was based around calming and desensitising Mary's lively mind and body. That said, Mary liked fun activities, so we quite often sang as we did our yoga together. Sometimes she found staying in static poses difficult, so we moved in and out of the postures, rather like limbering up. I already knew that Mary had a preference for rocking and circling movements, so we practised these. We counted rocking and circles from one to ten. Then we reversed the movements, counting again. Mary enjoyed this immensely; she nodded her head in time with my counting and occasionally made verbal noises in time with the numbers.

We developed a sequence of movements, focusing on stretching out the long muscles of the arms and legs, and also stretching and turning the back. When Mary did a seated twist, she looked carefully at me and then attempted the twist herself. I had to position myself so that she could still see my face when she moved her head. She found it very hard to do the postures without seeing me do them at the same time. I came up with the idea of drawing the postures on pieces of paper and letting her look through and choose which she wanted to do next. Mary was always very diligent about finishing the whole routine. As the days went by, I started to add new postures – still all on the floor, but including more challenging ones incorporating back bends and forward bends. I used the animal names for the postures, such as the Frog, the Snake and the Swan. Mary tried everything; she often giggled as she attempted new postures, keeping her eyes trained on me all the time. We did everything together, as a team.

After the seated postures, we moved to lying postures: bilateral twists and stretches. Finally, we lay on our backs, on the floor in *Shavasana*, the pose of relaxation. At first, Mary found it tough. Her natural sideways movement set her rocking from side to side and sitting up. She seemed uneasy on the floor and she watched me closely. I talked her through a 'body scan' (Carne, 2016), whilst lying on the floor myself. I closed my own eyes and gradually she became more still. Whenever I glanced across at her she was lying on her back, staring upwards towards the ceiling, gently dancing her fingers around on her stomach.

As the days turned to weeks, our routine became more sophisticated and elongated. Within a few weeks, Mary and I were doing well over an hour of yoga every morning. After the session, she was calm, she moved more slowly and quite often we stayed in the room at the top of the house. She looked out of the window and watched traffic passing, with no more urgency to investigate the house or disrupt things.

Communication

From engaging in the yoga with Mary, I started to recognise that she was making various attempts to communicate or at least join in with my verbalisations. I built up a very rudimentary library of pictures of objects and, on separate pieces of paper, the corresponding word. After Mary and I did our yoga session and she had had her break of looking out of the window for a while, I got out the pictures and words on the floor, right where we had done yoga together. Mary came over and showed interest straight away. I talked her through the pictures and words, matching them up and speaking the words as I went along. Mary immediately copied me after I separated them out again. She had watched the pictures and labels like a hawk and managed to match about 60 per cent of them first time. I now know that she probably saw both the pictures and the corresponding words as mainly shape and colour. Her immediate memory was so accurate that she was able to return them to their places with some certainty. She may have been as aware of a scuffed corner of a piece of paper as she was of the word itself. I never knew exactly how she was matching things up, but she enjoyed the task and it quickly became our second activity of the morning. Each day I was able to introduce new pictures and words. When she became confident at matching them, she sometimes also made verbal sounds and pointed towards items. I sensed that I did not particularly need to 'teach' her or reward her for getting things right. I kept my voice level and simply affirmed when it was correct or said 'try again' when it was not.

It seemed that Mary enjoyed the routine of the activity as much as showing her skills. She continued to watch me carefully when it was my turn and then diligently copy what I had done when it was hers. With some children who don't speak I have had a very strong feeling that they are desperate to do so. Sometimes they have shrieked, spat and grimaced in their attempts to be understood. Mary was different. She seemed very at home with herself. She looked at faces to understand what people meant and used her own body to show what she wanted.

Within two months, Mary and I had a whole morning of regular activities based around yoga and then various word and picture games.

After lunch, the residents of the home generally started to return in twos and threes. They were tired after a long day in their various settings and they tended to mill around in the communal areas. When Mary heard the doorbell ring she immediately charged downstairs to see who it was. She was very stimulated by new people appearing and tended to join them in their milling around. She grinned at the residents and swung from side to side as each person came home. I kept an eye on Mary at these times, as she found self-regulation almost impossible, but I couldn't be by her side at all times, as she often shot from room to room. One day, there came a loud cry of pain from next door and I went in to see one of the residents looking confused and upset as he nursed a red bite mark on his arm. Mary stood in the corner, gently swinging from side to side.

When you are a key worker with a violent or disruptive child, it is common for other staff to see you as a kind of extension of the child that you work with. Especially if another child gets hurt, their staff find it very hard not to place blame somewhere. As Mary and I were 'outsiders', it did not take long before we were seen in a rather negative light. It was politely suggested that in the afternoons we should stay on the upper floors of the house. Mary, however, had other ideas. She was drawn towards the hubbub downstairs. She liked to be in the thick of it and the staff in the home became increasingly anxious when she was mingling with the other residents. They looked to me to do something, but I knew from my previous experience that 'doing something' did not always go very well with Mary.

The outside

I decided that the best thing for all concerned would be to get Mary out of the house during this home-coming period. It was not forbidden – it just hadn't been recommended, and it was clear to me why: the general public are not very keen on getting bitten. Nevertheless, I decided to try an outing. At the bottom of the road there lay a towpath along a stretch of canal. Luckily, the canal was not very accessible from the towpath. I reckoned that it should be possible to keep Mary out of the water. About a quarter of a mile along the towpath, there was a bridge that crossed the canal, and from there another path led back to the house.

One day after lunch, we set off. Mary was wearing a bright red coat and was clearly excited. She started at a fast pace, straight legged, dropping from foot to foot. I virtually had to jog to keep up with her. She paused only to look at me and check we were going in the right direction. Within 15 minutes, we were back at the house. She shot in through the door, flung her coat from herself and stood in the lounge, swinging from side to side. I looked at her, and it dawned on me that she was more scared of going out than I was.

From then on, we went out for a walk every day. Once she became used to it, Mary slowed her pace and began to take in the scenery. When a boat appeared, she stood and danced her hands in front of her face as it passed by. People often waved from the boats and she immediately waved back and kept waving until the boat had disappeared. And then there was the issue of dogs. Mary, unlike some autistic children, rushed up to dogs and thrust her hands and face into their fur. Their owners would cheerily say, 'It's all right, he doesn't bite,' and I'd quietly think to myself, 'No...but she might.' In time, I was less apprehensive. It turned out that Mary had dogs at home and was very familiar with their ways. Although she handled them abruptly, they never seemed concerned.

As time went by, the walk, like our other activities, became routine. We tended to meet the same dogs with their owners and also the same boats. People said hello and Mary waved. At the top of the street was a small newsagent's shop. On my way to work, I went in and introduced myself to the owner. It was reassuringly quiet in there. I knew that Mary liked a particular type of small chocolate bar, so I bought one, ate it myself and stuck the wrapper to a piece of paper. The next day, I introduced the chocolate wrapper and its name to our morning session. Mary responded, and when we were on the walk I mentioned it again and led her to the newsagents. There was no one inside except the man behind the counter, but it was dark in the shop. Mary stayed on the threshold, peering in, probably trying to make sense of the strange environment. I went in and talked to the shopkeeper. He asked for Mary's name and called to her, but she wouldn't budge. After a few minutes, I suggested to Mary that we go, and we made our way back to the house. After that, every day we included the shop on our journey. It took about four attempts before Mary went in, but once she did, she immediately grabbed her favourite chocolate bar. We sort of jointly took it to the counter and she was out of the shop before I got the change. Over the next couple of weeks, she became more familiar with the environment, and she even took the chocolate to the counter with some money. It probably wasn't great for her teeth, but our walk was becoming longer, she was interacting with the community and, by the time we got back to the house, the residents had returned and settled down.

My time with Mary was only ever meant to be temporary. The social worker who employed me had in the meantime been working hard to find Mary a day placement. After two-and-a-half months, Mary left the residential home and went to a permanent day centre. The day that we parted, her father was quite emotional. Mary, however, just smiled, swung from side to side and walked out of the door without looking back, ready for another adventure.

REFLECTIONS ON MARY

This story of Mary is not directly about therapy. It is a story of everyday life and autism, and it's something that happens all around the world every day. It is very important for a therapist to intimately understand this world. The nuts and bolts of family life, getting through the day and regrouping for the next are central to those who have autistic children. I often suggest to parents of autistic children that they seek out other parents, because only they will truly understand the beauty and the hardship of living with their children. I personally am in no doubt that my years of work with autistic children and adults before I became a therapist was the best training that I could have had. A therapist has to be able to see beyond the therapy session and be honest in his or her enquiry about what that weekly session might actually mean to someone who has, for example, a significant learning disability. In Mary's story, we can see how events stack up; one thing leads to another, which in turn leads to simple, functional breakthroughs. It's difficult for a therapist to see all the events outside the session and what they might be leading to, which is why I always recommend that therapists who work with autistic children actively engage with the team that is around the child: because it's by working together that great strides can be made. As Mary and I made our simple and functional steps forward, how useful it would have been for me to report what had happened to a therapist. The therapist in turn could have built on that knowledge in his or her own sessions with Mary. At the same time, it would have been invaluable for me to have a therapist explain the underlying aspects of what was going on between Mary and me on a day-to-day basis. In this section, I hope I can bridge this gap, albeit rather belatedly. And the first thing that I would probably have told my younger self about was the three Ds.

The three Ds

The three Ds are: *distraction, defusing* and *de-escalation*. Because there is a developmental progression to the Ds, we will start with *distraction*.

With a very small baby, in order to stop her crying, we *distract* her by joggling her about, making a funny noise or getting her to look at something new. When it works, it's like magic. The baby stops crying instantly. Her mind has been moved away from her bodily discomfort and she is engaged with a new experience.

When children get to around two years old, they are no longer distracted so easily. They hold on to their unhappiness and if you, as a parent, persist in offering them a distraction, they will seize it from you and fling it across the room. They know what you are trying to do, and they won't have it. They want to stay with their emotion.

A parent needs to recognise that this is the moment to move on to the second D: *defusing*. This is best described as being like a bomb in those old cartoons: it's a huge, black, metal thing with a fuse fizzing away in the top. Now imagine what happens if someone removes the fuse. The bomb is still there, but it is no longer dangerous. In everyday life, defusing means to remove a person or object from a situation in order to avoid an explosion. For example, if the children fight in the back of the car, maybe one of them could sit in the front or they could sit in separate cars. This is defusing, because it removes or separates out the problem. A parent who relies on defusing needs to be very organised and needs to think ahead and plan how to defuse problems before they arise.

It's easy to see what the problem with defusing is. If everything is defused, no one ever learns how to cope with anything. If we arrange everything around our children to avoid any difficulty, they will not develop any coping strategies, which will cause problems later on.

At this point, we need to bring in the third and most variable D: *de-escalation*. This is all about becoming calm enough to cope with a situation. When we are de-escalated, we have the internal mind-space to think of solutions creatively. De-escalation techniques are many and varied. They range from having a hot bath, to bouncing a ball, to specific cognitive thinking exercises, but they all have one thing in common: they help create a feeling of spaciousness and self-awareness. When we are in this state, we are most likely to find solutions to the problem.

It is fair to wonder, why bother with the first two Ds? De-escalation is clearly the most 'advanced' of the three techniques, so shouldn't we solely use de-escalation as our technique? It's a rather beautiful fact that, actually, we use all three. TV, for example, is a classic example of a distraction. But there are legitimate times when all we want to do is to just sit and watch TV for a bit. There may also be times when we are having a serious problem, with addiction for example. When this is the case, any addiction expert will tell you that we can't have our drug of choice around us. We have to remove it completely from us; this is an example where defusing is the most helpful approach.

If we consider my problem with Mary in the cupboard, we can see that I didn't really utilise any of the Ds. I didn't try to distract her or de-escalate her, but there's a reason for that. I sensed that if I took a gentle de-escalatory approach, Mary would in the meantime unravel every toilet roll. However, once Mary left the cupboard, I shut it, which is a defusing tactic. What might have happened if I had tried to distract Mary? We don't know, but my guess is that she would have ignored it. The problem partly arose because others had no doubt taken a very strong defusing approach with her, for some considerable time. It's highly likely that Mary was never left alone with a box of toilet rolls. They were probably all kept out of sight and, as a result, when the opportunity arose with me, Mary was unable and unprepared to stop herself. In hindsight, it would have been useful if I had taken a more de-escalatory approach with my body. I put myself in a corner and directly in the line of fire. I could have at least said 'no' from outside the cupboard. That way, if Mary had come at me, she would at least have left the cupboard in order to do so.

There is another dimension to this scenario. The key is in how, throughout her two-and-a-half months with me, Mary constantly looked at me. It appears that to Mary I was something unfathomable. She was constantly looking at me as if trying to work me out. She was probably asking herself, 'Why does this "personthing" do this?' There was some anger when I stood in her way, but mostly she was just trying to get me out of the way. In showing her my injury, I was helping her. In that moment, I became less of a thing and more of a person, and she changed her behaviour with me for the rest of the day.

Yoga

Yoga is a form of movement and posture that has an inherent benefit to humans. It is the mindful enactment of shaping ourselves to the environment around us. When Mary engaged with 'hatha' (physical) yoga, she immediately appeared calmer. Although we were high up in the building, we sat on the floor and our bodies felt supported. She then experienced the lengthening and the releasing of her muscles, whilst in this held, floor-bound position. Bearing in mind that Mary used her eyes to get the vast majority of her information, these sessions were an excellent opportunity for her to watch me closely and slowly match her bodily movements to mine. For all of us, but especially someone who doesn't speak, this is communication.

Routines

When we look at the story, we can see how important routines were for Mary. In order to cope, her mother and father had kept her in a restricted environment; this, in turn, had influenced her and she herself had become restricted. When we are restricted, we tend to turn to routines more, to both comfort ourselves and make our limited lives feel more interesting. Parents and staff often come to me and describe a child who is immensely controlling; and usually, when we closely examine the situation, it becomes clear that their child may indeed heavily control, pattern and routinise some part of their lives, for example, in the family home. But control stops at the boundary of the home or their family members. Compared with other children who go out from the home and have wide social circles, their child actually has less general control of their lives. The restriction of a home-bound child tends to create a higher degree of control in the small circle within which they operate. The key with such situations is to encourage people outside their usual patterns and routines, so that they can experience a life with less control.

Mary habitually looked for the pattern in things and followed it. She and I created a patterned session of matching pictures and words. She enjoyed the structure and routine and therefore engaged in the learning. This has now become a standard method of working with autistic children; systems such as 'TEACCH' (Kirk *et al.*, 2009) deliberately use routines and structures as frameworks for enabling learning.

Within the structures and routines with Mary, there was a deeper schematic emerging. We discovered that Mary needed to go through a routine in order to move forward in her life. The first part of this routine was de-escalation. When Mary and I did yoga together, we were helping her to become calm. Being calm is the ground; nothing can be achieved without starting on calm and centred ground. Once Mary was calm and centred, her amygdala (the fight, flight or freeze centre in the brain) became less active, which in turn enabled her hippocampus to engage so that Mary could allow herself to think, pay attention and learn. This, in turn, led to increased confidence. When we think we know what's going on and we have achieved something, we feel much better about ourselves and we are more able to take risks.

So, finally, after calming, learning and then increased confidence, comes new endeavour. Mary was really very anxious when she went on her first walk. Even though it was not a great sensory challenge, it was an unusual experience. It's also entirely possible that Mary was herself worried about how she might behave. However, she did it and then went on to do more. She wanted to do something new and she managed it. This, as we can see, is because she had developed her own sequence of:

Calming, grounding (doing yoga)

Paying attention, thinking (matching images and words)

Confidence (feeling more able)

New experiences (going outside for a walk)

I lost touch with Mary after she went on to her new setting. It's possible that she forgot what we did together, and no doubt she went on to create many new routines and sequences as she went through her life. But this underlying process – which starts with calming and grounding and then goes on through learning and finally enabling new experiences – is strong. With help, I hope she kept it going, like a subterranean river that runs underneath the actual landscape of day-to-day activities.

In dance movement therapy, there are parallels with warm up, incubation and process models, which are used to describe how individuals and groups develop and move through a therapy session (Meekums, 2002). There is something essential in this developmental flow. Through our daily routine, Mary was able to rejoin her own developmental current and therefore join in with the wider routines of others around her.

PRACTICAL POSSIBILITIES

1. As a staff team or family, sit down together and discuss, write and draw which of the three Ds are your strongest and weakest. Try to mix and match your skills with the needs of particular children and activities. For yourself, make a commitment to practise whichever of the Ds you find hardest.

2. Actively think about your body positioning in relation to a physically unpredictable child. We all make mistakes, but if you find yourself repeatedly getting caught out in the same place or situation, change the way you do things. Stand in a different

place and move furniture and/or ornaments in order to keep everyone safe.

3. If you have an established visual timetable with a child, try adding a question mark (?) to a small part of it. Keep this time as 'unknown', but secretly prepare a simple but fun activity. This way we help children feel more positive and interested in the unknown and unplanned.

12

TIME OFF FROM MYSELF
Anxiety and Mindfulness

John was a talker. When he was on his own, you could see his lips moving and his eyes flickering as he held an internal debate. As soon as he was in company, those words became more audible and directed towards his companion. He talked quickly and with a lot of accuracy. There were not many gaps, except to elicit a response to a question. He was initially quite rewarding to talk with. He made sense and had carefully thought-out and interesting ideas. However, after a while, one started to notice how the conversation remained isolated around John's particular islands of interest. There was only minimal development on even his chosen subjects. The listener gradually realised that in the conversation, nothing that John was talking about had really changed in the last hour, day or week.

When John was little, it was seen as 'cute' that he asked 'funny' questions. To some extent, he was indulged, at least by people with whom he only spent limited time. It was clear to those who knew him better that there was a belligerence in his questioning. John seemed to be deeply curious about things and would question someone heavily to get an answer. But he wasn't necessarily that interested in a carefully constructed answer; he just wanted to get *his* answer. He asked the question to hear a predictable reply and thus complete a simple circuit of activity. John was curious, but ultimately his curiosity was overpowered by his fear. He was deeply anxious about many of the most basic aspects of life and therefore asked questions with predictable answers to help himself feel more secure.

I had come across John in a variety of situations, from when he was 11 to 14 years old, before I worked with him one-to-one as a therapist. I used to facilitate a dance and movement group with staff and autistic children in their early teens. John was part of it, but kept to his own agenda. The more the group moved around the room, the more urgent his questions became. As his voice matched the liveliness of movement in the room and the volume of the music, some of the other children started to shout, 'SHUT *UP* JOHN!' In the moments when I was able to focus more directly just on John, moving and talking with him, he became more contained. But this focused approach meant that the rest of the group had to drift along without my attention. I therefore decided to try a different approach. The group went into a gym, where they could engage with more individual activities, whilst still being together in the same room. John immediately scuttled up to the very top of the wall bars and stayed up there. His commentary about how he was not coming down eventually became a kind of background noise for the rest of the group as they did various physical activities, occasionally adding their own 'SHUT *UP* JOHN!' to the mix.

Once everybody had left the gym at the end of the session and there were just a couple of staff left, John descended with no great difficulty, talking the whole way down. The following week, John talked and talked about being 'upside down'. He span himself on the wall bars so that he could experience it. His floppy hair fell towards the floor as his gangling limbs shuffled around on the bar, trying to get a good grip. He didn't look very comfortable and he righted himself fairly quickly, but he kept talking about being upside down. Later, once everyone else had left, I asked John to come to a pommel horse. I helped him get on it so that his body was lying across it. He was comfortable and lying on his stomach. I suggested that he try being upside down now, and he put his head down. For the first time in the session, there was a short, blessed silence as he stopped talking. After a few seconds, he righted himself and immediately started talking about being upside down. In response, I said, 'You don't need to talk about it: *do* it,' and encouraged him to hang his upper body down again. Once again, there was silence. Once again, John righted himself and started talking about being upside down.

This carried on for about ten minutes. Every time John lifted his head up and started talking about being upside down, my response was to encourage him to actually be upside down. John then had another go and was silent. Eventually, when he righted himself and his usually pale face was tinged with pink, he said, 'How many days is it to the shortest day of the year?' I helped him off the horse and we walked back to his classroom, with at least a different subject to talk about.

More conversations in another place

A year or so later, I was asked to work one-to-one with John. He was becoming quite a burden to staff. They had to timetable themselves in rotation with him because after only a couple of lessons, they were becoming headachy and slightly mad with his constant chatter. Also, he was becoming more anxious and at the same time more risky. He was captivated by the idea of wrongdoing and tried it out, usually rather haphazardly. For example, he developed a fascination with what might be behind a door marked 'No Entry' or 'Private'. He was resolute in his attempts to immediately go through any door that prohibited his entry. Most of the time, the situation was no worse than just embarrassment for the staff who had to pull him back out of a kitchen or head teacher's office. But, once or twice, John found himself in rooms surrounded by moving machinery or tempting electrical switches and levers.

Finally, and most significantly, he suffered a bereavement in the family. A beloved relative had died of cancer and this turned John's formidable talking machine towards the subject of death, with no sign of any let-up.

I met with John in a quiet old sports shed next to the main building of the school. Around the shed was a small garden area with a pathway and a disused pond. It was a rather forgotten corner of the school, but for us it was perfect. There was no one around to be bothered by John's chatter, and the natural, low-sensory-arousal environment suited him very well.

Death and sex

When John came to see me, he had two subjects on his mind. The first was about his recently deceased relative. He repeatedly described the events leading up to his relative's death and then worked through the aftermath for himself and his family. Repeating the story did not necessarily help him to achieve 'closure', but he did seem to benefit from having a clear timeline about what had happened and when. This 'what' and 'when' information somehow took the place of the 'why'. Generally, after a bereavement, people ask *why?* I had noticed before that autistic people quite often focus instead on *what* and *when*.

As John told me about his relative in his last few months, he was reminded of a trip to a nightclub that they took together. Although John was under-age, he was allowed entry with his family early on in the evening. The event had a big impact on him. The sensory overload was powerful, but John found his wish to be part of the scene was stronger. He told me about the lights, the bass and the girls. When John looked at the girls in the club, he felt as though he'd stepped in through the TV screen. He had seen pretty girls dressed up and dancing, but always in a removed state, through a TV or computer screen. When he was at the club, John felt liberated by the simplicity of the situation. His verbal ability was irrelevant; he could just dance, and he did.

He and I created dance music with our voices and danced in the old sports shed. He was transported back to the nightclub, and he showed me how he had moved and then how the girls had moved. As a 15-year-old boy, he was amazed and fascinated by the women in the club. He told me about their clothes and especially their hair – the way it had moved and shone. He remembered every detail. If those girls had wanted to be noticed that night, they certainly were.

After a couple of weeks, once John was clear and comfortable about the privacy of our sessions, he told me about his sexual explorations. His fantasies were no more developed than simply remembering the girls in the club or others that he'd seen on TV, but he did have questions about masturbation. He understood what he needed to do and managed well enough from what he told me, but he was concerned about ejaculation. It disturbed him to have something coming out of his body and he worried about the mess to some extent; but, most of all, there was an anxiety about physically losing something and, indeed, losing control. Although he enjoyed sexual pleasure, he sometimes found the whole experience too intense in terms of his sensory integration.

We discussed whether he thought he could, at some point in the future, cope with having a partner physically close to him, but he thought not, reckoning he'd be too nervous and disturbed.

John talked to me about sexual matters most weeks. What he seemed to need most from me was to explore the possibility that he didn't have to masturbate according to the expectations that were around for teenage boys. Although he was not really part of a friendship group, he had still picked up a powerful idea that sexual behaviour was necessary. Over about three months, John seemed to come to terms with his sexual energy in relation to his sensory needs. He reported to me that now he masturbated only rarely, but he still enjoyed sexual thoughts when he was at home in his room. After some time, he no longer seemed to feel the need to discuss this aspect of his life with me.

The death of John's relative, however, did stay as a central theme for several months. As he talked through the death with me, he gradually started to fix on to more general themes about age (when one might die), time (how long we have) and change (what happens after death). These themes became strong areas of reflection for John and me. But, initially, the underlying issues were constantly clouded by a subtly changing array of questions. After listening to John's questions, I began to realise that they were too repetitious and scattered to be of any genuine use. It was hard to know which area to choose to explore. John's butterfly mind moved from flower to flower, but he was not stopping to drink the nectar from their centres. He needed some way to help him pause.

Inviting the bell

One of the best-known modern teachers of meditation is the Vietnamese Zen Master, Thich Nhat Hanh. He has written over 60 books and specialises in bringing simple but effective meditation practices into modern lives. He offers many techniques that may have been useful for John, but I decided to try three specific ideas. The first is known as 'inviting the bell' (Nhat Hanh, 2009, p.21).

I brought to our sessions a small, metal, bowl-shaped bell, which sat on a cushion and had a wooden hand-held beater about five inches long. First, I showed John how to invite the bell. This means placing the beater on the edge of the bell and producing a damped-down 'ting' sound. Thich Nhat Hanh describes this as 'waking up the bell'. Next, we breathe in. On the outbreath, once again the beater touches the rim of the bell. But this time, the sound is not dampened. The bell rings out freely as we deeply exhale. We then inhale and ring the bell as we exhale, twice more. Finally, we just sit quietly for several seconds, listening to the sound of the bell dying away and enjoying our breathing.

This practice is suggested as a simple and very effective way of pausing when we are engaged in the tasks of everyday life. It's a short and simple activity that sensitively brings us back to the present moment and gives us a chance to remember that we are living and breathing. It's used now by business people in meetings, school teachers in classrooms and children in their family homes. I wondered if it might be a useful way for John to collect his thoughts and questions by pausing his speech.

John seemed to find that the space the bell provided was helpful. He immediately latched on to it as a tool we could use. He asked me at the beginning of the session if I had the bell, and watched carefully as I got it out. There was no 'rule' about the bell. We just rang it when it felt appropriate, maybe three times in an hour's session. At first, I tended to pick up the stick to invite the bell if I felt that John was getting bogged down, over-excited or repetitive as he spoke. After a few weeks, John occasionally invited the bell when he felt he was losing himself in the labyrinth of his mind. One day, when we were together, he raised a particularly interesting question about the nature of time. I was, I thought, combining science and philosophy to give a full and involved reply. Just at that moment, when I realised that my own voice had been the only sound for rather too long, John reached out, took the stick and calmly invited the bell.

Pebble meditation

Some of Thich Nhat Hanh's practices were designed specifically for children. Pebble meditation is one such practice (Nhat Hanh, 2009, p.142). It requires four pebbles and takes about five to ten minutes. We place the pebbles next to ourselves and settle down into an upright but relaxed position. Then we take the first pebble. We look at it closely, examine its contours and textures and then breathe in and out three times whilst contemplating two keywords. One keyword is for the inhalation and the other is for the exhalation. Once we have completed this with the first pebble, we repeat it with the next pebble, and the next, until all four have been through the process.

Each pebble has its own two keywords:

1. Earth (inhale), Stable (exhale)

2. Flower (inhale), Fresh (exhale)

3. Water (inhale), Reflecting (exhale)

4. Space (inhale), Free (exhale).

This meditation is very simple and does not take too long. Someone with an attention deficit can usually cope quite well with it. The second useful aspect is that it is guided. If someone feels grounded by hearing a voice or is intimidated by silence, you can talk them through the sequence of the pebbles, from start to finish, pausing only in the intervals for breathing. Another aspect is that there is something physical involved – a child holds a real pebble in his or her hand, which helps to keep them connected to the natural world. This approach is deliberately elemental. We all understand the themes of earth and water. They have resonances for us that create a space for meaning to develop as we practise pebble meditation.

John preferred me to talk him through it. Even though he quickly learned the routine, he found it easier to stay with the activity if my words guided his mind. Generally, when John breathed in and out, he did so with very strong intention. His lungs worked like a bellows, expanding and making a loud sound as he exhaled through his mouth. I would often remind him to breathe gently through his nose and not to overfill his lungs or force the outbreath, but, when he practised pebble meditation, he just seemed to naturally breathe in this exaggerated way. He needed to feel the air coming in and out of his lungs strongly to get the necessary sensory feedback for himself, so that he *knew* he was breathing. Breathing in this way for mindful meditation is contraindicated, but I did not press him too much about it as he appeared comfortable, and he reported that he felt much calmer after practising pebble meditation. It became his favourite activity when we were together.

Adaptations

We had done pebble meditation for a few weeks, and I wondered if John might like to add his own themes to the ones from the original practice. John enjoyed this idea very much. We got used to going through our conversation that day and collecting the themes into pebble meditations. For example:

> Holding this pebble, as I breathe in, I think of my relative when he was alive. As I breathe out, I feel happy.

It took a while to consolidate John's rambling questions and ideas into simple, two-line meditations, but we managed it. Often the themes would be negative. For example:

> Holding this pebble, as I breathe in, I think of myself dying when I am older. As I breathe out, I feel scared of dying.

At first, I tried to encourage John to turn at least the second line of his meditation into a positive resolution. But he was adamant that he wanted his thoughts to be as they were. I respected his wishes and noticed that as he breathed in and out with his difficulties, he was somehow *placing* them. Yes, they were difficult and they weren't going away, but, by using pebble meditation, he was able to put them into the pebble and outside of himself. His questions eased off after we practised this. He became more relaxed. The question may not have been answered, but now he felt it had a home.

Walking meditation

The heart of Thich Nhat Hanh's practice is walking meditation. This is a practice enjoyed by many people from different cultures, in different ways. Thich Nhat Hanh would go on walks with sometimes many hundreds of people, all walking slowly and moving like a river. He explains that this practice is a way of connecting with our planet, and describes walking meditation as 'massaging the earth' (Nhat Hanh, 2009, p.14). When walking in this way, a useful way to focus the mind and the intention is to be aware of each step. When we do this, our pace generally slows. At its slowest, we inhale as we lift our heel and step forward, and exhale as we plant our foot back down on the ground in front of ourselves. As we breathe in and lift the foot, we can have a keyword, such as 'arriving'. When we exhale and place the foot, we can say 'home' to ourselves.

If the weather was good, John and I would come out of the fairly cramped shed and sit in the garden next to it. Sometimes, John was very lively when he arrived. His questions poured out indiscriminately and he leapt from foot to foot, chuckling as his mind raced on. At these times, we usually walked around the garden until his mind had settled enough to have a coherent conversation. It was a small area of about ten square metres, so we walked and indeed talked in a tight circle. On one side of the garden lay a paved area of half-metre, square paving stones aligned in a rectangular grid. From one side of the grid to the other there were about eight paving stones. At times, we hopscotched around on the slabs as we talked.

There were periods when John became seriously entrenched in both his questions and his view. When talking about time and space, he could be despondent. One powerful wish was to redo his entire school career – quite literally to start primary school again and go through the whole system. We discussed it at length. *Would he go back to being an infant?* John preferred the idea of staying as a young man. But he wanted everything else to stay the same. *Even the unpleasant experiences?* John contrasted his deep desire to repeat his life against the reality of change that faces us all, and found himself unhappy and uncertain.

I stepped over to the grid of paving stones and invited him to stand alongside me, both of us on our own square. In front of us were seven squares. I realised that this might offer a well-defined path for practising Thich Nhat Hanh's walking meditation. I showed John how to breathe in as he lifted his foot and then breathe out as he stepped onto the next paving slab. We repeated this seven times, until we got to the last square. For the first week, this was enough, but as the weeks rolled by it became, along with pebble meditation and inviting the bell, part of our routine.

Adaptations

One day, as we stood at the start of the grid, I thought about John's endless worries and about time passing and the relationship between life and death...and I wondered if our walking-meditation squares could somehow help with these huge issues.

I asked John to imagine that he was a tiny baby again, here on the first square of his life. Using the techniques of both walking meditation and pebble meditation, we breathed in and out whilst thinking about what John was like back then and what had been going on around him in his life. When he was ready, I suggested to him that he could decide what the next square might be. John immediately suggested nursery school, a pivotal experience for him. We stepped forward one step to the next square. Once again, we contemplated John's experiences and life back then. When John was ready, we moved on to primary school for the next step and so on.

John's new method of walking meditation took several weeks to develop. In each session, John refined the themes and also the timescales of each step. The death of his relative was always a square in its own right. It was a time for him when everything changed, and there was a loss of innocence. For some weeks, he struggled to get past this square. He couldn't take the next step. But, with encouragement, he began to make the eighth square where he was now, in the present moment. After some more time, John started to experiment with the idea of imagining himself in the future. He imagined himself older or married with children. Then finally, one day, he stood for a long time on a square envisioning his own death. But he was only on the seventh square. He looked at this next slab, then suddenly skipped onto it, exclaiming, 'And then I'll be born as another baby! Perhaps I'll be a girl!'

POSTSCRIPT

John was not the kind of person to have clearly defined endings. He tended to get somewhere and then go back to the beginning again. Our therapy progressed in a rather circular way. When he reached the end of his formal schooling and would have probably benefitted from a more practical and customised college placement, he instead insisted on staying at his school for a post-16 programme.

The programme was not really suited to him, and he was honest with me that he simply wanted to stay at school. He didn't want to change. For that year, we worked intensively in our therapy sessions on this central difficulty. He was faced with the harsh reality that although he had stayed in school to avoid change, change had happened anyway. His class teachers were different, the pupils were different and he felt miserable that he seemed unable to put off his impending adulthood. At times, John would simply bemoan his fate; he was deeply distressed that things had not stayed the same. He used his considerable brainpower to create schematics about the nature of time and the universe to show that things would all repeat again eventually. He got interested in reincarnation as a way of coping with his fear of change through death. At every turn, I gently reminded him that change and flux are at the heart of how we experience life. At these times, John relied on our three types of meditation more than ever.

In the end, he agreed that time was up on school and he had to leave. This meant that he would also be finishing with me, so we had yet more change to go through. Finally, John came to see me on his very last day. We had discussed it many times, tried to picture it and, now, it was here. For the first time ever, he didn't have much to say. We practised our pebble meditation and then walking meditation on the paving slabs. By now, he tended to do this practice without my help. He talked through each step as he took it. I started off alongside, but gradually fell back. I watched him as he took his final, eighth step into the present. After saying goodbye, he walked on, through the garden and back out into the school, to leave, for the last time.

REFLECTIONS ON JOHN

A person who works with autistic children needs to be able to dance his or her way between the practical and the impossible. For example, how do we deal practically with impossible demands from children who are in real distress? In John's case, he needed a fair bit of practical advice about sex and sexuality, coping with hyperactivity and so on. But at the same time, he also wanted to understand the impossible: Why does life have to change? Why do we have to die? What is the nature of time and space? Practical and impossible conundrums were completely meshed together for him. He frequently jumped from a big why to a small how and back again in the space of a couple of sentences.

Finding the real question

The first task was to get to the bottom of his continuous questions. If I had attempted to answer them all, I would immediately have become enmeshed with him in the impossible. We had to look at the nature of questioning itself to get anywhere.

Autistic children ask multiple questions for a variety of reasons. Four of the most common reasons are to:

1. know the answer

2. hear an answer that they already know, thus completing a circuit

3. try to make a conversation

4. be reassured by the answer.

When it comes to the first reason, we need to bear in mind that sometimes an autistic child may hear an answer but then subsequently lose it. I use the word 'lose', because it is somewhat different from 'forget'. Quite often, context may make an autistic child lose their knowledge. For example, a child might be able to toilet themselves with no problem at home, but in another setting they are not able to generalise about the objects around them. They are not able to see that a toilet is a toilet regardless of shape, colour or location. At these times, the child may 'lose' information and subsequently ask repeated questions. When this happens, the child simply needs to be told or shown again, perhaps several times, what he or she (theoretically) already knows. This is a practical skill that parents and those who work with autistic children need to be aware of. I certainly did answer John's questions many times and that was probably, to some extent, useful to him. However, he would get to the point where he was asking a question whilst simultaneously answering it. At that stage, we have to move on to reasons number two, three or four on our list.

The problem with children who are asking a question in order to fulfil a patterned behaviour, or those who are trying to make a conversation, is that it is hard to tell the difference between the two motivators. One way to find out is by the degree of interest that the child has in you as a person. If you don't fulfil the pattern correctly (answer the question in the way they expected) and they simply walk away, they are probably not trying to make conversation. If, on the other hand, they ask another question and another, they may have the genuine desire to talk with you. Unfortunately, their skills in this area are limited to asking questions, which makes for a rather 'monochrome' conversation.

John was really trying hard to converse with people or, more simply, to connect. He had high levels of anxiety about both the big things and the small things in life, but he was not especially worried by people. So, he looked to people to offer him reassurance. Whether I directly and practically answered his questions or not, I did always try to make sure that I reassured John. This means that regardless of what goes in or is lost in terms of verbal input, the child has a sense that they are safe with you.

John also experienced something else that we sometimes witness in autistic children who are loquacious: he seemed to have a sense that, if he spoke, the world around him became ordered. We can see this in many very young children as they first learn to speak. They create their worlds by talking about them and to them. It's cute in tiny children but less so in teenagers. John talked because of his high levels of anxiety. He really needed to be as sure as possible of his world. John experienced a lot of visual and auditory distortions and variations. When he spoke, his voice was a constant for him. The voices of others, even if they were unhelpful, helped him place himself in his world.

Space and time

I first had an introduction to John's particular relationship with space when he hung upside down in the gym. The experience, once I had managed to find a way to make it more comfortable, was so powerful for John that it restricted his speech. When he was hanging upside down, he was experiencing a strong influence on the vestibular system of his inner ear and on his overall sense of proprioception (the sense of where the body is in space) (Dickinson, 1979). It may just seem like a neat trick, but we can see throughout this story that John was searching for different ways to experience and stop his world. When he put his body in a different position, he saw things differently and found relief from his pressured and hyperactive experience of things.

John needed a sense of place and time. His experience of the world was so fluid that he verbally held on to anything and everything. How much this was necessary by the time he was into his teens is hard to say. John faced a dilemma. Life kept moving, and he couldn't make it stop. He understood that he needed fresh ways of thinking and being, but his self-created structure of talking and questioning was pretty much the only way he knew how to cope. Hanging upside down might be useful from time to time, but he needed a more permanent and on-going change of perspective.

I decided that the meditation skills outlined earlier in the chapter might serve as a replacement to the necessary holding-together that his talking was doing. I didn't try to stop him talking. That could, in fact, have been quite dangerous. Instead, I offered alternatives. The key with these alternatives, which John recognised almost immediately, is that they focus strongly on the safety of the here and now. Inviting the bell is a practice about understanding time. The ring of the bell delineates a small, manageable 'piece' of time for us to settle into. This is made more intimate by using the breath as a measure of the timing of the bell. So, the internal time zone of our breath meets the external time zone of the bell. They come together and we feel whole.

Pebble meditation puts us in touch with our environment. When we meditate on the themes of the earth, a flower, water and space, they are not abstract terms. The meditation invites us to feel each of these elements in the pebble and within ourselves. The earth contains the seeds for the plants and flowers; the water nourishes them and they grow up into space. A person with a confused sensory world needs these simple reminders about place. Wherever you practise pebble meditation, you can touch the earth and feel at home.

Walking meditation simply brings these aspects of time and space together into bodily movement. As we breathe in time with our steps, we touch the earth and feel in place. John had a lot of real and significant worries: he tried hard to resolve them through cognitive investigation, but his hyperactive and cyclical mind did not help him stay with any conclusions. For this reason, in both the pebble and walking meditation, we introduced his own personal stories. Breathing and walking presents itself beautifully as a two-step process. As I breathe in and lift my foot, I ask my question. As I breathe out and plant my foot, I arrive at my conclusion. Slowing this process down gave John a chance to breathe and just be with the dilemma. When we can do this, we can start to feel more at ease in not knowing.

The question answer

The Sufi poet Rumi says, 'Keep looking at the bandaged place. This is where the light enters' (Barks and Moyne, 1997, p.142). It's noticeable from John's story that his difficulties were, at times, almost insurmountable. I don't know if John read Rumi, but he certainly understood the reality of this line. When he was confronted with death, he went deeply into the difficulty it presents. Likewise, he was conscious of sexual issues and he brought them to me to be worked through. Quite often I have known staff make light of a child who, for example, wails mournfully about their favourite pencil snapping, but in truth we all know how the child feels. It is painful to walk this path of old age, sickness and death. The autistic child just has a particular view and, at that time, it is of their favourite pencil. But the dilemma is real. We all face it. It is life-shaped.

John showed much wisdom in how he faced adversity. Even though he was poorly equipped in some ways, he tackled all the big questions of life and from many different angles. A purely cognitive approach may have caused him to perseverate and loop his ideas and behaviours. John and I were able to combine traditional meditation techniques with personal creativity and physical movement and, as a result, he was able to ask real questions that had personal and deeply felt meaning. As he refined his questions, so he started to recognise that there is a two-step process. The question is itself, and it is also the answer. This can't be easily explained, but it can be experienced. On that last day, as I stood back, I watched someone stepping out on his journey. He had learned ways to be with uncertainty.

PRACTICAL POSSIBILITIES

1. Use a meditation bell at home or in the classroom as a way of creating a pause and a moment of quietness. Let everyone learn how to use it, and encourage the children to ring it occasionally.

2. Devise a time in the day when children can experiment with unusual body positions: upside down, balancing, curled up in a ball, etc. Let them find their favoured shapes and poses and also try others. Enable them to have fun with physical difference and share new perspectives.

3. With autistic children who talk incessantly, devise a gesture which means pause. Always allow the children to speak after the pause, and encourage them to use the gesture for themselves. Avoid making the gesture harsh or dominant (such as a flat hand up, meaning stop). Develop a gesture which is subtle and can be used at any time and in any place.

13

IN THE MOMENT
The Big Question

It had been a tough day: Neil's very first job interview. To tell the truth, everything had been planned in advance. The post was a temporary and voluntary one. I had plenty of discussions with the boss beforehand and I was confident that all Neil had to do was turn up.

Nevertheless, it was nerve-wracking for him – to be on the spot, hear the words, work out which ones form a question and then return his own words in the correct order. Neil had prepared all the answers, of course. He knew everything he needed to know about this short placement and a lot more besides. He knew the boss's birthday and so, of course, he knew what day of the week he'd been born on too.

In the end, Neil had done well. But he didn't always trust or quite understand what others said, so even when the boss affirmed that he had the job, it took a while to sink in. Neil was, in his quiet, restrained way, elated. We walked out of the venue together and got in the car. We were surrounded by beautiful countryside and a two-hour drive from home, so I suggested a walk up the hill.

The rolling hills fell away on either side of us. Green below and blue above. The path began to climb, and before long we found ourselves on a summit. The ground levelled out and, simultaneously, we stopped. All around was silence, except for the larks, rising and falling in a wide, clear sky. On the way up, as we walked, Neil had started to speak. Carefully, he went through the interview. What did he say? How did he respond? Was he all right?

'You must have been, Neil... You got the job.'

He fell into silence again.

'Jonas?' So rare to hear him call my name.

'Yes Neil?'

'Jonas, do *you* think I've got Asperger's syndrome?'

Suddenly, uncomfortable images from Neil's life appeared in my mind: his struggles with his peers, his teachers, his parents, himself and *that* word. That label, 'Asperger's', used to make him physically ill with denial. And yet, everyone kept using it.

That was all some years ago. The pressure had almost crushed him, and therefore no one had mentioned the word in Neil's presence for a long time. And now here it was, from Neil's own mouth, and high up in the hills. We had come a long way for this.

I didn't say anything for a while. What could I say that was neither a platitude nor too startling? How to fold the question back, so that Neil himself could find his own answer? Eventually, as he stood silent and expectant, I said: 'If it's useful or helpful for you to have Asperger's syndrome, then you can say: "I have this condition." If, on the other hand, it's not helpful to you...if it gets in the way of who you are, or who you want to be, then you don't have to use the label.'

Neil contemplated the huge landscape all around us. I knew that, whilst others embraced Asperger's syndrome, for him it had been like a life sentence, with no possibility of parole. He'd googled it, read books about it and fought with it every day of his life. And so, as we stood there together in the sunshine, he glanced at me.

'Are you saying that I can say I *don't* have Asperger's?'

'Look Neil, you are about to start a new job. Your boss appreciates that you may take longer to understand what he says to you. But the other people you meet on the job – the people who don't know you – to them you will be just like anybody else.'

Neil and I stood thinking about this, because in taking away a label, there can also be a loss of identity. If Neil wasn't an Asperger boy, then who exactly was he?

'So, I have a choice?'

I nodded.

Neil wasn't looking at me anymore. He was fixed on something in the distance, maybe something that I couldn't even see. I watched as the chronic tension in his shoulders softened a little. He seemed to get taller, more open.

'OK,' he said, and we started back down the hill, with Neil leading the way.

References

Adler, J. (1999) 'Who Is the Witness? A Description of Authentic Movement.' In P. Pallaro (ed.) *Authentic Movement.* London: Jessica Kingsley Publishers.

American Psychiatric Association (1994) *Diagnostic and Statistical Manual of Mental Disorders (4th ed.)* (DSM-IV). Arlington, VA: American Psychiatric Association.

Barks, C. and Moyne, J. (eds) (1997) *The Essential Rumi.* New Jersey: Castle Books.

Bartenieff, I. and Lewis, D. (1980) *Body Movement: Coping with the Environment.* New York: Gordon and Breach.

Best, P. (2003) 'Interactional shaping within therapeutic encounters: Three dimensional dialogues.' *The USA Body Psychotherapy Journal 2*, 1, 3–11.

Bogdashina, O. (2016) *Sensory Perceptual Issues in Autism and Asperger Syndrome.* London: Jessica Kingsley Publishers.

Carne, K. (2016) *Seven Secrets of Mindfulness: How to Keep your Everyday Practice Alive.* London: Rider.

Chodorow, J. (1991) *Dance Therapy and Depth Psychology: The Moving Imagination.* New York: Routledge.

Dickinson, J. (1979) *Proprioceptive Control of Human Movement.* New Jersey: Princeton Book Company.

Dodd, S. (2005) *Understanding Autism.* Sydney: Elsevier.

Edwards, G. (2005) *Sticking Arms, Sensitivity Drills and Explosive Fighting.* Basingstoke: Lexilore Publications.

Etherington, K. (2004) *Becoming a Reflexive Researcher, Using Ourselves in Research.* London: Jessica Kingsley Publishers.

GamePro (1995) 'VR headsets get warning.' *GamePro 84*, 140.

Grandin, T. (2009) *Thinking in Pictures.* London: Bloomsbury Publishing.

Kabat-Zinn, J. (1990) *Full Catastrophe Living.* New York: Random House.

Kiew Kit, W. (1996) *The Art of Shaolin Kung Fu.* Shaftesbury: Element Publishing.

Kirk, S., Gallagher, J., Coleman, R. and Anastasiow, N. (2009) *Educating Exceptional Children.* Belmont: Wadsworth

Lao Tsu (1972) *Tao Te Ching* (trans. G. Fu Feng and J. English). New York: Vintage Books.

Maguire, R. (2012) *Public Talk.* Oxford: Autism Oxford.

McMahon, L. (1992) *The Handbook of Play Therapy.* London: Routledge.

Meekums, B. (2002) *Dance Movement Therapy: A Creative Psychotherapeutic Approach*. London: Sage.

Mindell, A. (1985) *Working with the Dreaming Body*. London: Routledge.

Murray, S. (2008) *Representing Autism, Culture, Narrative, Fascination*. Liverpool: Liverpool University Press.

Nhat Hanh, T. (2009) *Happiness: Essential Mindfulness Practices*. Berkeley, CA: Parallax Press.

Pollard, T. (2012) *My First Makaton Symbols and Signs*. Harrogate: Tipi Publishing.

Richardson, M. and Friedman, N. (eds) (2007) *Clinician's Guide to Pediatric Sleep Disorders*. Florida: Taylor and Francis.

Richer, J. and Coates, S. (eds) (2001) *Autism: The Search for Coherence*. London: Jessica Kingsley Publishers.

Sansone, C., Morf, C. and Panter, A. T. (eds) (2014) *The Sage Handbook of Methods in Social Psychology*. London: Sage Publishers.

Scabbiolo, F. (2013) 'The Aesthetic Process' [talk]. Headington, Oxford.

Silberman, S. (2015) *Neurotribes: The Legacy of Autism and How to Think Smarter About People Who Think Differently*. London: Allen and Unwin.

Solomon, W. (2012) *Autism and Understanding: The Waldon Approach to Child Development*. London: Sage.

Stahl, B. and Goldstein, E. (2010) *A Mindfulness-Based Stress Reduction Workbook*. Oakland, CA: New Harbinger Publications.

Torrance, J. (2003) 'Autism, aggression and developing a therapeutic contract.' *American Journal of Dance Therapy 25*, 2, 97–109.

Trungpa, C. (2009) *Awakening the True Heart of Bravery*. Boulder, CO: Shambhala Publications.

Tustin, F. (1990) *The Protective Shell in Children and Adults*. London: Karnac.

Ueshiba, M. (1991) *Budo: The Teachings of the Founder of Aikido*. London: Kodansha.

Williams, D. (2006) *The Jumbled Jigsaw: An Insider's Approach to the Treatment of Autistic Spectrum 'Fruit Salads'*. London: Jessica Kingsley Publishers.

Yeo, C. J., Matthews, J. B., McFadden, D. W., Pemberton, J. H. and Peters, J. H. (1955) *Shackleford's Surgery of the Alimentary Tract*. Philadelphia: Elsevier.

Further Reading

Clements, J. (2005) *People with Autism Behaving Badly.* London: Jessica Kingsley Publishers.

Crimmens, P. (2006) *Drama Therapy and Storymaking in Special Education.* London: Jessica Kingsley Publishers.

Davies, M. (2003) *Helping Children to Learn Through a Movement Perspective.* London: Hodder and Stoughton.

Frith, U. (1989) *Autism: Explaining the Enigma.* Oxford: Basil Blackwell.

Gammeltoft, L. and Nordenhof, M. S. (2007) *Autism, Play and Social Interaction.* London: Jessica Kingsley Publishers.

Grandin, T. and Johnson, C. (2006) *Animals in Translation.* London: Bloomsbury.

Grandin, T. and Panek, R. (2013) *The Autistic Brain.* London: Rider Books.

Haythorne, D. and Seymour, A. (2016) *Dramatherapy and Autism.* London: Routledge.

Levy, F. (1995) *Dance and Other Expressive Arts Therapies.* London: Routledge.

Sherbourne, V. (1990) *Developmental Movement for Children.* Cambridge: Cambridge University Press.

Sherratt, D. and Peter, M. (2002) *Developing Play and Drama in Children with Autistic Spectrum Disorders.* London: Fulton.

Silberman, S. (2015) *Neurotribes.* London: Allen and Unwin.

Stern, D. (1985) *The Interpersonal World of the Infant.* New York: Basic Books.

Nhat Hanh, T. (1992) *Touching Peace, Practicing the Art of Mindful Living.* Berkeley, CA: Parallax Press.

Unkovich, G., Butté, C. and Butler, J. (eds) (2017) *Dance Movement Psychotherapy with People with Learning Disabilities.* London: Routledge.

Williams, D. (1996) *Autism: An Inside-Out Approach.* London: Jessica Kingsley Publishers.

Winnicot, D. W. (1991) *Playing and Reality.* London: Routledge.

About the Author

Jonas Torrance, MA, is a registered Dance Movement Psycho-therapist, a behaviour consultant and physical interventions trainer. He combines his therapeutic approach with a lifelong practice of yoga (qualifying as a teacher in 1984), martial arts (2nd Dan in 2004) and meditation (having trained with Zen Master Hogen Daido Yamahata for many years). Jonas first encountered autism whilst working in residential and day-care settings in the 1980s. He worked in specialist autism bases attached to mainstream schools in the UK for 25 years before becoming an independent therapist. As well as offering therapy to autistic children, he also facilitates training for teachers and parents, both in the UK and abroad.

Index